Sophia Willard Dana Ripley

CO-FOUNDER OF BROOK FARM

Sophia Willard Dana Ripley, 1803-1861
Collection of the Sisters of the Good Shepherd

Sophia Willard Dana Ripley

CO-FOUNDER OF BROOK FARM

by

Henrietta Dana Raymond

PETER E. RANDALL PUBLISHER
Portsmouth New Hampshire
1994

Submitted in partial fulfillment of the requirements for the
degree of Master of Arts in the Faculty of Political Science,
Columbia University.
June, 1949

Library of Congress Cataloging in Print
Raymond, Henrietta Dana
Sophia Willard Dana Ripley : co-founder of Brook Farm /
by Henrietta Dana Raymond
p. cm.
Originally presented as the author's thesis (M.A.)--
Columbia University, 1949.
Includes bibliographical references and index
ISBN 0914339-51-6
1. Ripley, Sophia Willard Dana, 1803-1861. 2. Brook
Farm Phalanx (West Roxbury, Boston, Mass.) 3. Transcen-
dentalists (New England) - Biography. 4. Spouses of clergy--
Massachusetts--Biography.
I Title.
HX656.B8R577 1994
335'.9744'61--dc 20
94-39485
CIP

Design: Debra Kam
Peter E. Randall Publisher
Box 4726
Portsmouth, NH 03802

Contents

Foreword

This is more than a biography of a very gracious lady by a very devoted historian; it is a chapter in American intellectual history.

It gives emphasis to ideas at work at Brook Farm a hundred and fifty years ago, and by inference to questions about our own troubled century. The facts are not new, but new is the emphasis and documentation.

Sophia Ripley, wife of a Unitarian minister of Boston, was a "high-minded," "blue-stocking" Transcendentalist (there was a club of such "intellectuals"), and a founder with her husband of Brook Farm, a "utopian" community designed to deal with the ills of the time. After the Farm's "demise," she became a convert to Catholicism. Her conversion might simply be attributed to her personality, except that conversion was also true of other people of both sexes (one thinks of Arthur Schlesinger, Jr.'s, *Orestes Brownson*). Another such convert, Isaac Hecker, a one-time baker at Brook Farm, even became a priest, and a founder of the Paulist Fathers. Were such persons fatigued, or frustrated, or seekers of security, or persons simply fed-up with their social philosophy?

Their era was a "fermenting" period in our history with plenty of "utopian" communities around (Sophia Ripley even visited one in Ohio), with women's rights to the fore, etc., but there was also plenty of "anti" thinking - anti-Masonry, anti-drinking, and of course anti-Popery. Perhaps a gentle religious mantle fell over life at Brook Farm. It had a chapel, and all religious beliefs were respected. These "intellectuals" must often have been opposed to the "anti" thinking of the time.

Brook Farm is rich in social and intellectual history, although it must be admitted that its finances were always shaky and that the great fire of 1846 did finish things off. It may have been something of a success, especially in education, in spite of Hawthorne's weird *Blithedale Romance*, which angered Emerson at the time, and which a century later gave a field day to the admiring D.H. Lawrence.

Are we in for a similar "fermenting" time, today? The "utopian" interest is perhaps not so keen, but the women's liberation movement would surely please Margaret Fuller, and the "back to nature" movement may be identified with modern environmentalism. This has been a century remarkable for change. We are perhaps less optimistic about the nature of mankind (see Reinhold Niebuhr's Gifford Lectures, *The Nature and Destiny of Man*).

This is a work of devotion as well as of great documentation. Mrs. Raymond is a Dana, as is her subject. She is also a Catholic, as her subject became. This book is her M.A. thesis at Columbia University. Not to read it is unthinkable.

Robert A. East
Retired Professor History
The City University of New York

Author's Note

We Americans sometimes oversimplify our economic history. In addition to our capitalistic tradition, we also have a tradition of cooperatives and of socialistic experiments. Historian Arthur Bestor counted two hundred such experiments before the Civil War. He included both secular and Protestant religious groups. One could add to these Catholic monasteries and convents.

Sophia and George Ripley founded one of the most interesting of these experiments, Brook Farm in West Roxbury, Massachusetts. It was remarkable because of the intellectual distinction of many of its members and visitors, including Nathaniel Hawthorne, Ralph Waldo Emerson, Elizabeth Peabody, Margaret Fuller, Charles A. Dana, Orestes Brownson and Isaac Hecker (later founder of the Paulist Fathers) - Elizabeth Peabody wrote of it in *The Dial* II, no. 2, October, 1841 in an essay called "A Glimpse of Christ's Idea of Society."

The Brook Farmers tried to combine "plain living and high thinking" and to make their lives consistent with their thought. They ran a farm, a newspaper called *The Harbinger*, and a school in which both adults and children participated in an informal way - star gazing at night to discuss astronomy, etc. They especially tried to combine physical and intellectual and artistic work.

I want to thank Professor Henry (called Harry) Wadsworth Longfellow Dana, who during his last years of life introduced me both to Sophia Ripley and to Brook Farm. I am also beholden to my friend, now dead, Lisette Riggs Isely, who shared her knowledge of the Ripleys. The Massachusetts Historical Society helped by for letting me spend happy hours copying manuscript letters and guiding me as I went. I am also grateful to Houghton Library at Harvard for access to Emerson's correspondence and Margaret Fuller's, and to the Paulist Fathers' for access to their archives relevant to Isaac Hecker.

Finally, I want to thank my husband, Irving Woodworth Raymond, who, in a marriage of 30 years, encouraged me to study and write. I also thank my five daughters, especially Elizabeth Ellery Bailey, who made possible the publication of this book.

Henrietta Dana Raymond
York Harbor, Maine
August 1994

Preface

There is renewed interest in Brook Farm. In 1988, the site was acquired by Boston's Metropolitan District Commission. Archeological research began in the Spring of 1990. An interpretive plan for the site is currently being developed.

So it is timely to publish this biography, even though it was written 45 years ago. Sophia Willard Dana Ripley is, in the words of Professor David Herbert Donald of Harvard University, an "almost forgotten heroine of the Brook Farm experiment." The history of Brook Farm is related through the lens of this woman, an active participant who was committed to its vision. Her story is told through the use of primary source materials, mainly letters. It would be hard to duplicate today the scholarly effort of the author, my mother, who undertook to locate, organize and then properly date these letters. After the death of Harry Dana (see Author's Note and many of the footnotes), the letters have been distributed even more widely among various historical societies, as well as university and religious archives. The biography is presented as it appeared in her 1949 Master of Arts thesis at Columbia University. The photographs have been added (only the portrait of Sophia herself was included in the original thesis). The Index is also new.

The careful use of primary source material, particularly unpublished source material, is important. For example, my mother came across published material that depicted Sophia Ripley as "sneering" at her husband George who was suffering from a cold. The interpretation seemed to my mother to be unlike the total portrait she was finding from her research, and she sought out the original letter. She discovered that Sophia also had a cold and was "sneezing." A number of later authors on Brook Farm (see the excellent bibliography by

Joel Myerson, *Brook Farm: An Annotated Bibliography and Resource Guide*, New York: 1978) have reprinted the "sneering," which gives a highly misleading impression of this woman. She did not sneer at all. The portrait presented here, of a woman who was very much an idealist, motivated by issues, is praised by Joel Myerson as "the best biography of Mrs. Ripley."

I gratefully acknowledge the assistance of a number of people. Chermaina Roundtree retyped the manuscript onto computer disk at her home, after hours, and proved to be an excellent sleuth in locating some of the photographs. Valerie Belmonte, a work study student, was most helpful in her bibliographic searches. Matina S. Horner, former President of Radcliffe, located the current leadership of the Roxbury Historical Society and wrote the opening commentary. Her enthusiasm for the manuscript, which she describes as "an inspiring story" that captures "a remarkable moment of greater Cambridge and Boston social and intellectual history," has been heartwarming. Professor Robert A. East wrote the thoughtful Foreword. Professor David Herbert Donald provided advance commentary. Rose Safran provided practical suggestions as did Peter Randall. Institutions and individuals whose archives and collections provided the photographs includes:

Boston Public Library (MA)
Columbia University Library (NY)
Joel Myerson (SC)
Massachusetts Historical Society (MA)
Paulist Fathers (NY)
Radcliffe College (MA)
Sisters of the Good Shepherd (NY)
Sterling F. Delano (PA)
University of Illinois Library (IL)
West Roxbury Historical Society (MA)

I am particularly grateful to Professor Will Holton, who graciously permitted us access to the collection of the West Roxbury Historical Society and to Sterling F. Delano who gave us access to the slides he had taken as part of his exhibition on Brook Farm in 1991 at Villanova University.

Elizabeth Ellery Bailey
University of Pennsylvania
August, 1994

Costume Worn by the Women of the Brook Farm Community
Collection of the West Roxbury Historical Society

I
Childhood

When Sophia Willard married Francis Dana Jr. on August 4, 1802, Cambridge society may well have nodded its head in approval of a very "suitable" match. Francis was the son of Francis Dana, Chief Justice of the Massachusetts Supreme Court and former minister to Russia. There he had tried to persuade Catherine the Great to recognize the United States. Catherine refused, but entertained him unofficially, and he came home an honored citizen.[1] Sophia was the daughter of President Willard of Harvard—a stiff and unbending old autocrat who insisted on the Harvard students and instructors doffing their hats to him when they met in the Yard. The irrepressible Washington Allston, who was a friend of the young Danas, had amused himself as an undergraduate (1798) by caricaturing President Willard with his great white neck cloth sticking out in front and his great wig sticking out behind. Another sketch, also supposedly of President Willard, places him side by side with Napolean Bonaparte.[2]

Unfortunately this marriage, so socially desirable, turned out unhappily. According to family tradition Francis Jr. was "no better than he should be" and did not support his family.[3] He and his wife had four children—two daughters and two sons.

The elder daughter, Sophia Willard Dana, the subject of this essay, was born on July 6, 1803.[4] Francis lived extravagantly and speculated heavily.[5] Then he left home, traveling to Russia, Germany, India, South America and the western part of the United States.[6] He left his family saddled with debts. In 1811 his wife filed a request in court for a guardian for her children.[7]

The details of this family tragedy have been lost in the mists of time. Vague references are to be found in the letters, written many years later, by his daughter Sophia. There is also a memorandum dictated in 1890 by Ruth Charlotte Dana, Francis' niece and Sophia's best friend. She said:

> Judge Francis Dana, when his son, Francis Dana, got into financial difficulties through speculation, took the two eldest grandchildren, Sophia and Mary, to live with him. He himself had lost so much money through his son's speculations that he had to diminish the number of his servants and kept only one horse and vehicle. The aunts, Martha, Betsy and Sarah, washed, dressed, and taught the little girls, and did the ironing as only one washerwoman could be afforded. Before this time the son, Francis Dana, had lived in a handsome house in Pemberton Square in Boston during the winter, and in summer used to have an out-of-town house, at one time occupying the Brattle House in Cambridge with its large gardens. At that time he kept a horse and carriage. Yet he did not pay for all these things and his father was obliged to settle for his son's bills.[8]

The old Chief Justice died in 1811 and the question arose what to do next. Charlotte Dana's memorandum continues:

> After Judge Dana's death, the trustees for his will very mistakenly advised the heirs to sell the Dana Mansion—the beautiful large house which he had built on Dana Hill in Cambridge—the furniture and everything, so as to settle up all the son's debts at

once. Since the sale was a forced one, it did not bring much. It would have been better for them to have stayed on living in the house and to have paid off the debt gradually. In that case the house might have been still standing; for it was through the negligence of the new family that came to occupy the house that hot ashes were left in a barrel at night and the house was burned down....

It was found necessary to break it gently to the wife of the extravagant younger Francis Dana that something would have to be done in the way of economy. Accordingly, an intimate friend of the family, Dr. Jackson,[9] went to see her, and offered to take her daughter Sophia who was a friend of his own daughter, to spend a year in his Boston home and to go to school there with his daughter. He then suggested to Mrs. Francis Dana that since she was one of the few ladies in Cambridge who owned a piano, and who was an accomplished player, he would find pupils for her if she would be willing to give piano lessons. She refused indignantly.

Apparently giving piano lessons was beneath the dignity of a daughter of the President of Harvard College.

It is not clear from Charlotte Dana's memorandum what happened the next few years to the two little girls, Sophia and Mary Elizabeth. Perhaps they were with their mother. Perhaps they were with the aunts, whom Sophia in later years would refer to as "my three mamas."[10] Perhaps Sophia did go to live with Dr. Jackson. She is said to have graduated from Dr. Park's School in Boston.[11] In any case her childhood was clouded with all manner of sorrows. Two of the aunts, Aunt Sarah and Aunt Betsy, were engaged to be married to two brothers named Foster. The Foster brothers came to visit the Danas, caught an epidemic which was then raging, and both of them died. Aunt Sarah also caught the disease which left her an invalid all her life. Sophia's uncle, Richard Henry Dana Sr., poet and future founder of the *North American Review*, sickened too and was never really strong afterwards.[12]

This same uncle Richard had married a "beautiful and graceful" young lady, Ruth Charlotte Smith. According to her daughter, she embroidered, painted, sang and played on the guitar. Apparently her gifts as a housewife were less conspicuous. An amusing story throws light upon her and upon the "Aunts":

> ...while the Richard Henry Danas were living at the old Vassall house...Henrietta Ellery, later Mrs. Channing, went to tea. She was then fifteen years old and going to school in Cambridge. She told Mrs. Dana's sisters-in-law, Aunt Betsy and Aunt Sarah Dana, that she had been invited to tea by Mrs. Dana. They seemed very unsympathetic and said, "Like as not she will forget the butter." Sure enough Mrs. Dana did forget the butter and had to send over to Aunt Betsy's for some.[13]

In 1822 this engaging aunt of Sophia's died, leaving four small children. Aunt Sarah, Aunt Martha and Aunt Betsy then jumped into the breach once more and moved in with him to take care of the little ones. Not long afterward the family was furthered saddened by the death of the baby, Susan, as the result of a fall. The remaining three children were Charlotte, Sophia's lifelong friend, Richard Henry Dana Jr., future author of *Two Years Before the Mast*, and Edmund Trowbridge. Sophia must have seen a lot of these cousins. In her letters of later years she speaks of their father as "Pa," of the Aunts as "my three mamas," and of Charlotte as "my little sister."

In 1822 Sophia Dana graduated from Dr. Parks' School in Boston. She apparently determined to make her family self-supporting. Her two brothers, Joseph and Francis, lived with the Aunts and went to Harvard. But she and her mother and sister took a little house in Mason Street, where the Radcliffe

gymnasium now stands, and there Sophia opened a school—
boarding and day. Many of the "best" families in Cambridge
seem to have sent their daughters to her. Sophia did most of
the teaching. Her sister, Mary Elizabeth, taught dancing and
"superintended the girls' manners," helping out in the class-
room now and then. Later, finding the house too small, they
moved to 94 Brattle Street (the old colonial Vassall House, the
same the R. H. Danas had lived in) and later still to Fay
House, which in those days was called "Castle Corners," and
which is now the administration building of Radcliffe College.
Two little boys were admitted as a special privilege to this
girls' school. One was Sophia's cousin, Edmund Trowbridge
Dana. The other was James Russell Lowell.[14] Lowell, writing
about this experience in 1838, described Sophia Dana as "a
very learned and accomplished woman." He studied Latin and
French with her and "there were no thrashings at all."[15] An
amusing description of Lowell as a student at this school was
recorded by Miss Elizabeth Ellery Dana in 1900, from information she had just received from her aunt, Charlotte Dana.
"My aunt says 'James Russell Lowell and Edmund went to
school to Sophia in the brick house (Fay House) and had a
stool each side of Sophia at the head of the table in school.
Jim wore embroidered ruffled shirts with cuffs. His sisters
took care of him and I of Ned.'"[16]

Besides teaching the children, Sophia gave historical lectures to women which, according to Justin Winsor's *Memorial
History of Boston*, "were highly enjoyed by her pupils."[17]

On August 22, 1827, Sophia Dana was married "in the oval
room" of Fay House[18] to Reverend George Ripley, a promis-
ing young Unitarian minister. Ripley had written of her to his
sister as "the being whose influence over me for the year past
has so much elevated, strengthened and refined my character."[19] Sophia engaged Miss Elizabeth McKean to take over
the school, assisted by Mary Elizabeth Dana. After two years
the school was given up.[20]

Sophia Dana School at Castle Corners (later Fay House , Radcliffe College, ca. 1900)
Collection of Radcliffe College

II
The Minister's Wife

What did Sophia Ripley look like at the time of her wedding? We do not have any description of her at this period. But we do have descriptions of a much later date, and a black and white portrait done shortly before her death in the winter of 1860–61.[21] One of these descriptions, written by her niece Isabella Dana, gives an extraordinarily vivid impression of personality:

> You ask for particulars about Aunt Sophia's appearance, and mention her height. Yes, she was very tall, but so graceful in her movements that there was no awkwardness from her great height. She seemed to float through a room, and a friend asked one day "Don't you suppose Mrs. Ripley has a knob concealed under her dress that she touches with her foot to make her skirt fall in such graceful lines when she sits down?" The two words I heard oftenest applied to her were "stately" and "elegant," and I once heard a young man say that he felt proud to be seen walking on Fifth Avenue with Mrs. Ripley. After she and Uncle George had found their feet financially after

the wretched disasters of Brook Farm, she began to dress quite beautifully. A friend expressed some surprise in the change from the severe simplicity she had formerly advocated. She replied that George wished her to dress well, and that it was by no means a trial for her to do so, as she really cared for dress. I once heard Miss Julia Metcalf say that Mr. Ripley seemed to look on her as an idol and loved to hang ornaments upon her....

I never heard her called handsome and she probably was not so. But there was something so lovely in her face, that the effect was somehow the same — perhaps the English would have called it *countenance*. Her exquisite manners, and her low, beautifully modulated voice, added to the charm and her reading to me as a child was a rare delight. To this day I often recall whole sentences from those stories, and the very inflection of her voice.

Aunt Sophy had very beautiful hands, even after the disasters of Brook Farm. One day, long after her death, I happened to meet a lady who had lived at Brook Farm and told her of my mother's dismay on finding Aunt Sophy washing the heavy working shirts of the laborers. "Oh," the lady said, "that state of things had to be stopped, as her poor little fingers were so injured that they had to be bandaged...

I could write about Aunt Sophia all day and all night, as she is as vividly before me as when I last saw her, and she continues to be one of the great enthusiasms of my life.[22]

Other descriptions of Mrs. Ripley tally with this one as to height and grace. They add that she was blonde.[23] Her portrait shows a strong face, with luminous eyes and a kind mouth. Aesthetically the face is marred by a very long nose. As for manner, two descriptions speak of her as vivacious,[24] one as reserved.[25] She must have been rapid in her motions. Marianne Dwight's letters from Brook Farm speak of Mrs. Ripley as "running."[26] And Sophia speaks of herself in the same way.[27]

Apparently there had been difficulties in the way of George Ripley's and Sophia Dana's marriage. Perhaps the problem was who would keep the school going for the support of Mrs. Dana and Mary Elizabeth. Perhaps the couple were waiting for George to be appointed to a church. Some "most unexpected" events happened to make the marriage possible. Perhaps one was the news that Sophia's father was coming home. In any case he did return the year of her wedding, and in 1829 was a member of the Massachusetts Legislature.[28] Another fortunate event may have been the invitation to George Ripley to preach at the Purchase Street Church. Whatever the difficulties and the solution, George had written to his sister Marianne in May, 1826:

> In your last letter you asked me what were my prospects on the subject which was nearest to my earthly happiness; then I should have answered, all was black darkness. Now, my dearest Marianne, by a most unexpected train of events, the obstacles to our affection are removed; a just regard to prudence does not forbid us to cherish an attachment which has long been the secret idol of our hearts....My father may, perhaps, think that it would have been more prudent for me to have deferred this consummation until my prospects in an uncertain and trying profession were more definite. To this I have to say, my wisest friends assert that my prospects of professional success, in the highest sense of the term, are tolerably fair, — so much so as entirely to justify this arrangement....It has never been my wish you all know, to be a rich man, nor what the world calls a great man, but to be a respected, useful, and happy man. And this connection, which is founded not upon any romantic or sud-

den passion, but upon great respect for intellectual power, moral worth, deep and true Christian piety, and peculiar refinement and dignity of character, promises, I think, to advance me in the best way in this life, and to aid me, above all, in the great end of life, the preparation for heaven.[29]

It would seem that Dr. Jackson was still keeping an affectionate eye on Sophia's affairs, for George ended this letter:

My mother will recollect her great admiration of Dr. Jackson. You will inform her how deeply he is interested, how valuable his friendship, how paternal his advice.

Frothingham gives a description of George Ripley in the 1820's so suited to the earnest young author of the above letter that one cannot but smile to read it:

Well does the writer of these lines recall the vision of a slender figure wearing in summer the flowing silk robe, in winter the long dark blue cloak, of the profession, walking with measured step from his residence in Rowe Place towards the meeting-house in Purchase Street. The face was shaven clean; the brown hair curled in close, crisp ringlets; the face was pale as if with thought; gold-rimmed spectacles concealed the black eyes; the head was alternately bent and raised. No one could have guessed that the man had in him the fund of humor in which his friends delighted, or the heroism in social reform, which, a few years later, amazed the community. He seemed a sober, devoted minister of the gospel, formal, punctilious, ascetic, a trifle forbidding to the stranger.[30]

Nevertheless, the "fund of humor" seems to have been abundantly present in the married life of the Ripleys. Sophia sparkled with it too. These two had a way of laughing at and with one another that would help them through many a difficulty.

For the next dozen years the lives of the Ripleys were comparatively uneventful. A series of letters from Sophia Ripley to her sister-in-law Lydia Hobart Ripley,[31] with occasional notes from George appended, reflects the usual routine of a minister's wife. Sophia received numerous callers, attended to household tasks, betook herself on errands down "little dark alleys where my duties often lead me."[32] There were frequent visits from the Ripleys and from Sophia's sister, Mary Elizabeth. Sometimes George arranged an exchange of pulpits to enable him to visit his family in Greenfield for a while in the summers. Sophia had a flair for gossip. She recounts engagements, weddings, births, tidbits about mutual friends, anything that strikes her as amusing. Sometimes the news was more somber. During the epidemic the winter of 1828–1829 she tells of many deaths. Then she adds:

> …though we have been more with the dead than the living this past week; and have been called to sympathize with bereaved friends—yet within our happy dwelling—everything has been sunshine as usual—I hope this uninterrupted happiness will not make us feel as if it belonged to us as a right or make us less prepared for misfortune. -"which comes to all"—I think, at times, I fully realize, that it cannot last long or this world would be too dear to us—but the thought does not cloud my present enjoyment—it only seems to render it more precious.[33]

In this same letter Sophia says that she is "making slow but sure progress" in German and drawing. As for George, "every moment that he is not writing sermons or making parish visits or poring over a book—he has pen in hand for the Register." The article which he wrote for *The Christian Advocate* on Transubstantiation has been reprinted in an English periodical. She refers to the "wicked" Andrews Norton whom she contrasts with Samuel J. May of Connecticut, who preached for them yesterday and who believes that "kindness will subdue even wild beasts—and certainly it will men."

In June of 1830 Aunt Martha Dana married Washington Allston. On Wednesday, August 4th Sophia wrote:

> …Yesterday we had a delightful visit from Aunt Martha & Elisabeth—They both made very particular enquiries for you. Last week Mr. Allston finished a beautiful picture of a lady reading—the day it was done he invited Mr. Harding—& one or two other friends to come & dine & see it—they all approved—& Aunt M- pronounced it the happiest day of her life.[34]

The Monday before the Ripleys had walked out to Cambridge to call on Aunt Betsy where:

> ….George was introduced to Mr. Adams[35] for the first time -& made out to take tea very comfortably by his side—& if you can realize it—allowed me to walk to the port arm in arm with him.

On Tuesday, November 2nd [1830] Sophia wrote again of the Allstons:

> …we passed last Friday most delightfully in Cambridge—took tea & passed the eveg at Mrs. Allston's with a family party—Coleridge was the theme of our discourse—[36]

On Sunday Emerson had preached for George Ripley's congregation:

> …& after that—will you tell Marianne—I will accompany her all lengths in her admiration. His sermon was above all praise—no language of mine could do it sufficient honour. He took tea with us afterwards—& I really thought I discerned some glimpses of feeling piercing the stern & unbending rigidity of his manner.

The fall of 1830 George Ripley went to Baltimore as visiting minister, stopping off in New York and Philadelphia. Sophia actually formed the "magnanimous resolution" of sending two of his letters on to his family "with sketches in his off-hand masterly manner of the people he met."[37] However, George, on his return home, wrote that on no account could the letters go out of the house because of "the great liberties taken with individuals."[38]

In January 1831 Sophia's younger brother Joseph died out West. In February she wrote to Lydia:

> All our dear Joseph's friends—were advising him to propose himself as candidate for the office of District Attorney—The latter part of November he went to New Orleans "that valley of the shadow of death" upon this business -where he must have received the seeds of the disease which proved fatal to him— though he left there in perfect health & visited his friend Hedge on his way to Judge Winchester's— They parted in high spirits congratulating each other that they had passed unimpaired through their first unhealthy season in this climate. The next news Hedge heard was of his death; which happened a very few days after they took leave of each other. Every circumstance which reaches us…is full of consolation—but all consolation is insufficient; except the one thought that He who sitteth on the throne of the Universe cannot err—I can submit & say with sincerity "Thy will be done"—but this does not give me composure—I can banish the recollection of our loss for a season—by the thick crowding duties & cares of life—but then, at intervals, it rushes over my mind with such intense anguish that human language cannot describe it & no words from human lips can console it—[39]

Sophia had been trying to comfort her mother:

> …Most of my time during the first fortnight has been
> spent in Cambridge with our afflicted parents….Moth-
> er is very well—& has acquired a tranquillity that I
> thought she could not attain for months; though she
> can never recover from her loss. He was her youngest,
> her darling—the dearest object of her affection—& no
> pleasure in life was so great to her as expecting &
> receiving his letters & looking forward to meeting him
> again—which we all did with too much confidence—

This letter also told of the death of Mrs. Emerson (Ralph
Waldo Emerson's first wife):

> …our sweet Mrs. Emerson passed away from us like
> a beautiful vision—She rode out on Sat—& expired
> early on Tuesday—She was perfectly sensible of her
> situation & spent the night before her death—in con-
> versation & prayer with her family. There were few
> present at her funeral except those who knew & loved
> her—The rooms were filled with the most beautiful
> flowers—arranged with exquisite taste—which had
> been sent her during her illness. Mr. Ware officiat-
> ed—it was the anniversary of his own wife's death—
> & he preached for Mr. E—the following Sunday—

On February 6, 1832 Sophia noted a visit of Henry
Wadsworth Longfellow's to Boston, soon after his first marriage:

> …we feel truly grateful that nothing has happened to
> prevent our full enjoyment of his friend (i.e. George's
> friend) Mr. Longfellow's visit who is certainly one of
> the most delightful specimens of human nature I ever
> met with. Tomorrow he & Mrs. L—leave town, & we
> meet them for the last time this eveg- at Miss God-
> dard's, whom you have not forgotten. There have
> been no large parties-during several weeks—but
> numerous small ones—Two or three of an eveg-Little
> suppers etc. Many of which we have attended.[40]

III

Transcendentalism

George Ripley was a faithful Unitarian minister—with the double leaven of liberalism and democracy working within him. For him the minister's job was not to *instruct* his flock, but to *seek truth with them*. He was seeking it within himself too, and earnestly studying philosophy trying to find a basis for certain knowledge. For George Ripley lived through and experienced in himself the transition between the sensationalist philosophy of Locke and the new intuitive school of the Germans. One of his friends at Harvard, F. H. Hedge, had studied in German universities. He and George Ripley became two of the most scholarly apostles of German thought in New England. They felt a true Romanticist distaste for a philosophy that pretended that all knowledge came through the senses. The most vital and exalted kinds of knowledge, they thought, the moral urge and the quest for God, were innate in the human heart. Some of their friends, including Emerson, Margaret Fuller, Bronson Alcott, Elizabeth Peabody and others felt the stimulus of the new thought. They formed themselves into a club which became known as the Transcendentalists. Its first meeting was at the home of the Ripleys.[41] They decided to publish a magazine called *The Dial*.

George Ripley, 1802-1880
Collection of the West Roxbury Historical Society

In his enthusiasm for this new philosophy George Ripley began to edit a series called *Specimens of Foreign Standard Literature*. For Americans who could not read foreign languages this series was an important introduction to European culture.

It seems quite likely that Sophia Ripley did some dipping into her husband's philosophical library, which was a remarkably fine one. She was an able linguist and a steady reader. From remarks in her letters she seems to have followed her husband's writings closely. In any case her own writings show decided ease in seeing philosophical implications. She is reported to have been an eager member of the Transcendentalist Club.[42]

Meantime the new philosophy was brewing dissension among Unitarians. Dr. William Ellery Channing, a saintly and winning leader of the Unitarian movement, in his able attack on the Calvinistic doctrines of total depravity and predestination, had laid it down as a principle that human nature is essentially good. The vistas he opened up of the possibilities of infinite perfectibility for mankind were one of the inspirations of Transcendentalism. But Channing, while denying the Trinity, believed nevertheless that Christ was divine in a sense similar to that used centuries earlier by Arius. He was a special emanation of God, and existed before His earthly life. Moreover His message was divine. Unitarian professors at Harvard were teaching variations on this comparatively orthodox kind of Unitarianism. They wanted to keep revealed religion, using human common sense as a guide to what was really revealed. Now this new generation came along convinced that human intuition was the only revelation necessary. Christ was divine only in the sense that He was more attuned to the Divinity than most men. Ministers like Andrews Norton were shocked at what seemed to them the retirement of the Transcendentalists from all objective tests of truth into the inner fortresses of their own subjective intuitions. Norton launched an attack against the heretics. He posited the miracles of Christ as proofs of the authority of his mission. A heat-

A

FAREWELL DISCOURSE,

DELIVERED TO

THE CONGREGATIONAL CHURCH

IN

PURCHASE STREET,

MARCH 28, 1841.

———

BY GEORGE RIPLEY.

———

[PRINTED BY REQUEST, FOR THE USE OF THE CHURCH, NOT PUBLISHED.]

BOSTON.
———
1841.

A Farewell Discourse Delivered to the Congregational
Church *in Purchase Street, March 28, 1841 by George Ripley*
Collection of Joel Myerson

ed controversy followed. George Ripley wrote several articles for *The Christian Examiner* defending Transcendentalism. A high point in the debate was reached after Emerson, who had resigned his ministry in 1832 because of conscientious scruples against the service of the Lord's Supper, delivered his famous "Address to the Harvard Divinity Students." This was not only frankly naturalistic, it was also pantheistic.[43]

But the Transcendentalist Club did not confine itself to abstract philosophy. The members were tremendously interested in the application of philosophical principles to human society. The depression of 1837 had been severe and prolonged. Misery and suffering were appalling. The members of the Club began to discuss whether an economic and social setup in which such things could occur was right in principle. Could it be possible that a society based on the principle of competition of brother against brother was the realization of Christ's kingdom on earth? Could individual men realize and develop the God within them when they were exploited and had no time left for education, for intellectual and artistic activity, to unfold the beauty of their minds?[44]

One ardent member of the group became impatient of the endless discussions. Of what use were theories unless they were put into practice? "Mrs. Ripley," wrote Theodore Parker in his journal, "gave me a tacit rebuke for not screaming at wrongs and spoke of the danger of losing our humanity in abstractions."[45] That for the future fiery reformer, Theodore Parker!

In 1838 George and Sophia Ripley took a trip out West and Mrs. Ripley visited the German communistic colony of Zoar in Ohio. She wrote a letter about it which was later published in the Transcendentalist magazine, *The Dial*,[46] and republished by Horace Greeley in *The New Yorker*. Her impressions are interesting in view of the principles the Ripleys would later advocate in their attempt to form an ideal community at Brook Farm. She wrote:

We may see fine scenery, but nowhere in our country

such easy countenances, free from care, and so pic-
turesque a population. Every individual gives a smil-
ing greeting, and even the young girl driving her team
speaks in a gentle musical tone.

This absence of strain Sophia attributed to the fact that "no
one is hurried or busy, though all are employed." The people
were "laboring tranquilly and leisurely without any appear-
ance of task work." Much wasteful duplication of effort for
the women was avoided by the use of community kitchens and
nurseries:

> The women here are as much at leisure, so far as
> household affairs and tending children is concerned,
> as the most fashionable lady could desire; for the
> cooking is done at one large establishment, where
> they go to eat, and have every variety of country fare,
> but are allowed meat only twice a week, and their
> children are taken from them at three, and put under
> the care of matrons, the boys in one house, and the
> girls in another, till they are old enough to be of use,
> when they tend cattle, mow, reap, or do any other
> kind of field work. They have no task set, at least
> among the older members, but each does the most he
> can out of doors and in.

Sophia did not think communism suited to all natures:

> ...all the young persons, who were bound to them, at
> the end of their apprenticeship prefer the risk of self-
> support with independence, to the safe and tranquil
> but contained mode of life of the community; and as
> they are permitted to leave if they choose, are many of
> them enjoying their flourishing farms in other parts of
> the State, probably prizing the little word mine more
> than any in their native tongue. The children of the
> settlers usually remain....

Discipline was simple. People were put on probation for misbehavior. If it continued they were banished from the community. The children were well cared for and lived in neat, airy dwellings. They seemed happy and healthy. She was pleased to discover "clean and abundant wardrobes" of the little girls, "with a closet full of little colored muslins, and white linen caps, with white frills for their Sunday wear." But she noted, "I rather think they receive very little education at any season."

She would have liked to have seen more culture:

> We visited the mill used by the community, after we had examined the landscapes and flower pieces of the head man of the place, a very old person and self-taught, whose devotion of his leisure hours to the fine arts, and the triumphant exhibition of them by our guide, were productive of more pleasure to us, as indicating some love of culture, amid all the toil of their active lives, than we could obtain from the works themselves.

She would also have liked more democracy. The government was paternalistic and the leader "...receives visits like a king, and it is evidently his policy to keep at a dignified distance both from his own people and strangers." His "countenance is striking, decided but calm, with a full grey eye, very mild in its expression" but "he evidently is nothing of a philanthropist, and this lessens our interest in the community."

On Sunday, February 9, 1840 Sophia Ripley wrote a letter to John Sullivan Dwight, a young friend of hers and of her husband. At this time he was a young preacher, very sensitive and shy. Later he joined the Brook Farm community and still later he became a famous music critic, and editor of *Dwight's Journal of Music*. She called her letter a "journal" of the week since Dwight's departure for his church at Northampton. It is interesting for its picture of the life the Ripley's were leading at this time. It is also much more self-revealing than the letters to Lydia Ripley. This is true of all her letters to Dwight, whom she seems to have found a congenial spirit:

> ...Sat—a severe snowstorm all day & in the eveg; very unfavorable for our journey but not so for our retirement & tranquillity. Little Franky[47] was not so much out of the way when he said "Aunt Sophia can't I get up to heaven on the snowflakes when they are falling." Heaven seems gently to descend in the quiet influences of their silent fall. I can't resist the desire to go out in a gentle snow-storm, so I walked forth in the afternoon & "caught" a severe fall—It shattered me sadly, but wonderfully was I consoled, on looking up to find myself opposite the temple, where no one could look out the window & laugh at me. Sunday on account of this accident at home all day—reading Balzac's Cesar Birotteaui—It is the history of a per-fumer—& his misfortunes. An honest & good soul conquered by circumstances, his wife is a beautiful character, & here & there are exquisite touches of ten-der feeling—but the author to show us that he is at home everywhere, fills one volume with the details of a bankruptcy & various mercantile transactions, impossible to be idealized, I take it by the most imag-inative; certainly not on paper, if they may be in action.[48] Anna Domini was faithful to us in the eveg—but C. P. C.[49] not so. Wholly unacquainted with the notes Ambrosianae of Bedford Place, he thought it too late for roasted potatoes after the Oratorio. As if there could be any more fitting close to the Creation than a specimen of the first plant cultivated by Adam in Paradise. Monday was a day very like other days—no golden & no iron hours— I spent the eveg with my friend Mrs. Alvord[50] whose grief like that of every true person, is a per-petual teacher....The weather became so severely

cold that George was seized with a rheumatism this eveg—which has kept him crouching in an arm chair by the fire all the week, enacting the octogenarian, & he assures me with his usual optimism that it is not nearly so dreary & disagreeable to be old as one is apt to imagine. Tuesday was a most cruel cold day—a day when it is hard to keep up a cheerful spirit even in a cheerful home. You spent it I know stretched on the hearth rug before a great fire—the side not next the fire freezing—reading the narrative of some voyage to the North Pole—indulging the most self-willed skepticism—not doubting the existence merely of goodness happiness & friendship—but denying that there is anything good in goodness—happy in happiness or friendly in friends. In all this my sister Marianne[51] (who is now below reading the third head of your sermon) would most deliriously sympathize. We were cheered in the eveg by a most interesting description of yr first Sunday's preaching at Northampton; its success, effect on various individuals etc. Weds came, & with it Margaret's[52] 2d course of conversations—This opening one was crowded by the world's people, the curious, feminists? etc.; so that we who belong there could not talk & Miss F— had to address the assembly, which she did very well, though by no means doing justice to herself. In the eveg- came Mr. E's—[53] lecture on education, which though much better than anyone else could have done was only the less of his best things—The same we had before in a slightly altered dress. I am not sorry the lectures are drawing to a close, for he is tired of them & their life is departing. Though you & I voted the last soiree, a bore, the same persons had the temerity to come again; & truly we had a very pleasant eveg—Mr.

E[54] told stories about steamboats running races with lightening etc. After these noisy folks had gone C. P. C. seated himself at the piano, & indulged, or rather expressed for us in song the melancholy feelings called up by your absence — selecting the Vale of Avoca — tho' I leave thee now in sorrow, & other doleful ditties. We are all going to Dr. Channing's[55] next Wednesday eveg after lecture & Mr. Rolker is to be invited Thursday eveg was a large party at the Waterston's. George not able to go on acct of extreme decrepitude, & I had to throw myself on the charity of friends. Mr. Felton[56] was there in his merriest mood, & various other persons of yr acquaintance. Friday passed the day on one side of the fire-place sneezing. George the other groaning — & not having sufficient musical ear to harmonize these expressions of suffering, the discord was horrible. Sat spent in much the same way; but in the eveg, in a fit of desperation I put on my hat & went to the concert to hear Russell,[57] Knight Ranger etc — & now, my friend, I should rave — but I well remember your reproachful looks whenever I indulge in such aberrations. I must however just say that for the first time I was ashamed of Boston; that men feel authorized so to insult her, and that she should enjoy it. Fortunately no good music was profaned. Knight sang Russell's songs & Russell Knights. The verses I presume were written by themselves — for there was a harmony in the ignoble union of words & music which quite reconciled my musical taste to both. R— sang the maniac in a very dramatic manner, & thrilled one with horror — but it is just the style which no man of musical soul would ever have recourse to; & his attempts at the pathetic with his coarse voice & person had the effect of road farce. Kendal's clari-

onet solo was the only approximation to music during the eveg I think I never saw such a throng of
people of all sorts collected on such an occasion.
This is not raving I hope.

I hear of nothing new & have read no very interesting thing this week. Coleridge's literary remains will
hardly come under that category. George is better
today, went to Dorchester & Mr. Hall preached for
us—I have been to church during the writing of this
letter—don't you perceive a break somewhere & a
burst of higher inspiration. I wish I could tell you of
an amicable dispute between Father Taylor[58] & Mr.
Bartel[59]-in which to all B's representations of the lectures—Mr. T- would answer—Emerson has it in him
& you haven't—he isn't turned on a crank as you all
are by yr people—A man who is perfect as he can be
is a Christ—I am amazed to find you a scholar don't
know that.

I hope on acct of my gossipy letter you will not be
unwilling I should close by calling myself as ever—yr
friend

—S. W. R[60]

Two weeks after the writing of this letter Sophia Ripley's
mother died.[61] The following summer, perhaps to give her a little vacation after this shock, the Ripleys went to board at a
milk farm in West Roxbury. Mrs. Ripley wrote about it to
John Sullivan Dwight:

My dear & revd. friend

No dearer for being revd—I should have considered that person my enemy who had told me, when we
parted in May last that two months would pass away
& no letter pass between us; but you are moody, &
have a respect for the moods of others (which is not
the case with all moody persons) & will therefore
readily excuse my silence when I tell you that I have

not felt at all like writing since I have been here. Only three letters have dropped from my pen, & those in a regular fit of desperation, which is by no means a genuine source of inspiration. That I have neglected to send you a word of remembrance must seem quite inexcusable, & my apparent forgetfulness justifies you entirely in closing yr last letter to George without a line of kind regards to me; not even the good set clerical phrase "remember me to your excellent wife, or my best respects to good Mrs. Ripley;" but John, never give up yr faith in old friends. I sent you a message of great length in George's first letter & will you credit it? he finished & sealed it without inserting one word of it. Wasn't this too cruel? And what was worst of all he was so penitent that I could not scold him for it.

What a luxurious life you are leading this summer. For most of us it would be too enervating; but if it does not create a distaste for work, it will be a most glorious preparation for it. We too have been leading a life of extreme self-indulgence in the most positive retirement. Our farm is a sweet spot, which I will not describe, for I trust we shall see you here before the season is past. I am not at all disappointed in my expectations from seclusion, for even my lonely hours have been right ones, & in this tranquil retreat I have found that entire separation from worldly care & rest to the spirit which I knew was in waiting for me somewhere. We are nearly two miles from any creature, but one or two quiet farmer's families, & do not see so many persons here in a month as we do in one morning at home. Birds & trees, sloping green hills & hay fields as far as the eye can reach- & a brook clear running, at the foot of a green bank covered with shrubbery opposite our window, sings us to our rest with its quiet tune & chants its morng song to the rising sun. Many dreamy days have been my portion here—

roaming about the woods, or lying half asleep under the nut trees on the green knoll near by—or jogging along on my white pony for miles & miles through the green lanes & rural roads which abound in our neighborhood—where you meet no well dressed gentlemen & ladies taking their afternoon airing, & hardly a solitary hay-cart or foot passenger—Even George lies for hours on green banks, reading Burns, & whistling to the birds who sing to him.[62]

They had walked over to Margaret Fuller's the evening before to hear some music. "It was refreshing to the spirit to hear a strain of inspiration from Beethoven again—the first since you left us." The first number of *The Dial* was just out:

> …We are heartily rejoiced that you like "the Dial" so well. George, Margaret & Theodore all run it down unmercifully—It has not fire & flame enough for them; but the reflected approbation of the public makes them more truly to appreciate it now. It is thought by many, myself among the number, a very charming book. Miss Peabody says "it is domestic, giving the everyday state of feeling & thought of the writers, there is no effort about it, & much strength behind….

Later in the same letter Sophia referred to Theodore Parker's sermons:

> …I wish you could have heard some of Theodore's heretical sermons this summer. They are truly grand—fearless, solemn even beautiful. He is creating a stiff breeze about him—but do you not see how all these holy words are only the echo & application of what our band has been silently dropping out for three years past—which have sunk deep, taken root, & budded in the glowing breasts of our more practical men?

This summer of 1840 was a turning point in George Ripley's life. In May, during the visit to Northampton mentioned in Sophia's letter, he wrote to the proprietors of the Purchase Street Church suggesting that since the finances of the church were precarious, perhaps they might prefer to do without his services. On October 1st he wrote to the parish as a whole explaining that as things stood he could not serve as their minister with a clear conscience.[63] He had to open his mind freely to them. To him Christianity meant something wider and deeper than the conventional sermon on Sunday, that avoided the new philosophical interpretations of God and man, and that avoided moreover the question of social reform. Christianity should be a leaven that should renew the face of the earth. Wars and the use of force should disappear before the power of Christian love.[64] Punishment should be replaced by the reformation of the individual and prisons become hospitals. He did not want to be a priest dogmatizing to his people. He wanted to be their equal and brother. If his parishioners were out of sympathy with his aims and beliefs, and pained by his "heresies," then he wished to resign his ministry. On January 1st he sent in his resignation, to take effect the 1st of April.[65]

In April of 1841 George Ripley and his wife and his sister, Marianne, and a few other friends moved out to Brook Farm, the same farm at which the Ripleys had boarded the summer before. They set to work to found an ideal society. On May 6 Sophia, in Boston to close up her house for the last time, wrote to John Sullivan Dwight.[66] She and George found the skepticism of the public in regard to their venture very annoying, but "our friends sometimes annoy us still more, by speaking of our enterprise as one requiring high, heroic valour, whereas, it has never seemed to George & myself anything but the simplest, most every-day affair possible." One cannot but gasp a bit! A thirty-eight-year-old minister and his wife throw up his life career and set out to found Utopia—and she calls it "the simplest, most every-day affair possible!"

The description of the parting with George's parishioners is quite touching. One senses how intolerable any "false" relation was to Sophia:

> Parting with Parish (this entre nous) has been the
> hardest, because we could not feel—as the kindest
> among them seemed to feel, that they were losing
> their all. Tearless we saw tears flowing all around
> us—& yet we never loved them all so much—loved
> them better for their weeping—but the relation was
> false—to each & all, & every parting tear was the
> righting of it, & seemed more like an invigorating
> dewdrop than an emblem of mourning. Many sub
> stantial proofs of kindness, & farewell letters were
> delicately offered in the most affecting way—a few
> gentlemen presented us with nearly $500—& the
> most beautiful garden tools to a large amount.

Garden tools! Carlyle, whom George and Sophia Ripley
admired so much at this time, has often been quoted for his
humorous description in *Past and Present* of George Ripley and
his Brook Farm Friends as "Socinian ministers" who "quit
their pulpits in Yankee-land...and retire into the fields to cultivate onion beds." But his remark a few lines later has been all
too frequently ignored: "to make some nook of God's Creation
a little fruitfuller, better, more worthy of God; to make some
human hearts a little wiser, manfuller, happier—more blessed,
less accursed! It is a work for God."[67]

Brook Farm., ca. 1937
Collection of Sterling F. Delano
Original in Bestor Collection, University of Illinois Library

IV

Brook Farm: Trying to Actualize the Ideal

Sophia Ripley, in her letter of May 6, 1841, described to John Sullivan Dwight the earliest days of the Brook Farm experiment:

…More of laughing than of weeping we have had the last few weeks, for a busy & merry household we are at Brook Farm—where George has been planted, or rather planting for the last month, & where I find myself the larger half of the time, for my heart is there, & beckons me continually. Next week I lock the door of No. 2—& cross the beloved threshold for the last time—of that dwelling, where we have enjoyed deep but very hard-earned happiness. We feel established & perfectly at home in the country, & our relations to each other are so natural & true that they seem to have existed always. The number assembled around the table in our large kitchen is thirteen & will soon be number sixteen....Hawthorne is one to reverence, to admire with that deep admiration so refreshing to the soul—He is our prince—princely in everything—yet despising no labor & very athletic & able-bodied in the barn yard & field....[68]

The housework was "light compared to my city labors" and "all of us are agreeably disappointed in our physical powers — particularly George — who does a harder day's work every day than the last, & feels better than ever before." Sophia had been reading Carlyle's *Heroes and Hero Worship*:

> …Have you read Carlyle's last book? Isn't he a hero? Will you with my love ask Charlotte Blake to read his account of Mohomet & see how surprisingly it harmonizes with what has been said in *our little* basement concerning him. I am now proud of being a Mohometan.

Apparently these early Brook Farmers were very much in earnest about shaking the dust of "the world" from their feet:

> …our intercourse with the world is mainly by letter, for we don't hear from town oftener than once in a week, & have voted not to tell each other the news, if we know any.

Curiosity, however, sometimes got the better of them: "I wish you could see the scribbling in our little parlour of a rainy day!"

At first Brook Farm was known as "the Ripley Community" and George Ripley made himself responsible for it. Ripley had explained its aims to Emerson in a letter in November 1840. He wanted:

> to insure a more natural union between intellectual and manual labor than now exists; to combine the thinker and the worker, as far as possible, in the same individual; to guarantee the highest mental freedom by providing all with labor adapted to their tastes and talents, and securing to them the fruits of their industry; to do away with the necessity of menial services by opening the benefits of education and the profits of labor to all; and thus to prepare a society of liberal,

intelligent, and cultivated persons, whose relations with each other would permit a more wholesome and simple life than can be led amidst the pressure of our competitive institutions.

To accomplish these objects, we propose to take a small tract of land which, under skillful husbandry, uniting the garden and the farm, will be adequate to the subsistence of the families; and to connect with this a school or college, in which the most complete instruction shall be given, from the first rudiments to the highest culture.[69]

In the fall of 1841 Ripley's community became "The Brook Farm Institute of Agriculture and Education." The Articles of Association are interesting.[70] Each member was to hold one or more shares of stock. But regardless of how many shares he held, each member was entitled to one vote. The property of the Association was vested in four trustees and administered in common. No member could be held personally responsible for losses incurred by the corporation. And any member might withdraw from the Association upon a year's notice. In that case he was entitled to withdraw his capital and interest. Each shareholder was entitled to five percent interest on his stock per year, but not to more. Instead of interest he could receive tuition for one pupil in the school. Besides this fixed interest there were to be labor dividends. At a subsequent meeting it was determined that members were to receive board in return for their labor. If they labored only half time, they should receive only half board and must pay for the rest. Or they might pay their entire board themselves, if they chose not to labor for the Association. All types of labor were paid equally, on the principle, as Elizabeth Peabody wrote in *The Dial*:

> that as labor becomes merely bodily, it is a greater sacrifice to the individual laborer, to give his time to it; because time is desirable for the cultivation of the

Constitution of
the Brook Farm Association

Articles of agreement and Association
West Roxbury, Mass
between the Members
of the
Institute for Agriculture
and Education

In order more effectually to promote the great purposes of human culture; to establish the external relations of life on a basis of wisdom & purity; to apply the principles of justice & love to our social organisation in accordance with the laws of Divine Providence; to substitute a system of brotherly cooperation for one of selfish competition; to secure to our children & those who may be entrusted to our care the benefits of the highest physical, intellectual & moral education which in the present state of human knowledge the resources at our command will permit; to institute an attractive, efficient & productive system of industry; to prevent the exercise of worldly anxiety for the competent supply of our necessary wants; to diminish the desire of excessive accumulation, by making the acquisition of individual property subservient to upright & disinterested uses; to guarantee to each other forever the means of physical support & of spiritual progress; & thus to impart a greater freedom, simplicity, truthfulness, refinement & moral dignity to our mode of life; — We the undersigned do unite in a voluntary Association, & adopt & ordain the following Articles of Agreement & Association, to wit

Art. 1 The name & style of this Association shall be the Brook Farm Institute of Agriculture & Education. All persons who shall hold one or more shares in the stock of the Association & shall sign these articles of agreement, or ficial duties.

Art XVII The Association may from time to time adopt such rules & regulations not inconsistent with the spirit & purpose of these articles of Agreement as shall be found expedient & necessary.

Geo. Ripley.   Boston

Sophia R. Ripley

Saml. D. Robbins

D. Mack   —   —   Cambridge

Maria Mack

Marianne Ripley

Nath Hawthorne

Lemuel Capen

Warren Burton

Minot Pratt

Maria J Pratt

Geo C Leach   —   Gloucester

Mary E. Robbins

Francis D. Farley.

Chs Anderson Dana.

Sylvia Allen

1842.
Feby 17.
"   "

intellect in exact proportion to ignorance. Besides, intellectual labor involves in itself higher pleasures, and is more its own reward than bodily labor.

Another reason, for setting the same pecuniary value on every kind of labor, is, to give outward expression to the great truth, that all labor is sacred, when done for a common interest. Saints and philosophers already know this, but the childish world does not; and very decided measures must be taken to equalize labors, in the eyes of the young of the community, who are not beyond the moral influences of the world without them.[71]

A six-day working week was adopted with an eight-hour working day in winter, and a ten-hour day in summer. Sick members were entitled to support and to medical and nursing care.

These articles seem to have been the result of much thought. They are especially interesting to us in their relation to Sophia Ripley's comments in her "Zoar" essay. Provision was made for the personal freedom that comes from private ownership. Members could own property of their own and need not invest their all in Brook Farm. Moreover they were free to withdraw. But the attempt was made to secure the advantages of communism. The farm and school were held in common, and in working one was contributing to the common good of all—*not* each man for himself and Devil take the hindmost.

Moreover, there was to be no task work. Labor was to be paid by the hour, and hours, by standards of the nineteenth century, were short. Perhaps one of the most interesting concepts developed at Brook Farm was the concept of the work hour as the medium of exchange.[72] A controversial point seems to have been the right of members to pay board instead of laboring. Elizabeth Peabody in *The Dial* hoped that this would not be allowed.[73] Perhaps it was allowed as a compromise to keep the money of board-paying members. Perhaps because of belief in freedom and dislike of coercion. Perhaps simply out of recognition, from experience as well as from philosophical conviction, that all natures are not alike and that for some men participation in routine labor can destroy creative ability. Nathaniel Hawthorne—"our prince"—had already found it impossible to shovel manure and milk cows and still write.[74] But he remained for a while longer in the Association and was even elected trustee and Chairman of the Committee of Finance.

As in the case of other constitutions, the way in which the Brook Farm constitution was put into practice was of more significance than the document. Mr. and Mrs. Ripley and the other leaders tried to set an example of service. George Ripley took upon himself the tasks of milking the cows and cleaning the stables. Sophia washed the kitchen floor and worked long hours in the "muslin room" at washing and ironing.[75] George P. Bradford, a cousin of Emerson's, and George Curtis, future editor of *Harper's Magazine*, used to help with the washing and hanging out the clothes.[76] This Ora Gannett Sedgwick later wrote "seems to me more chivalrous than Raleigh's throwing his cloak in front of Elizabeth."[77]

George Bradford himself, looking back in later years at his Brook Farm experience says that he thinks the most valuable contribution of Brook Farm was its democratizing influence on its members—the meeting on terms of equality and friendship with people of most diverse backgrounds.[78] One of the members was a former cook of the Danas, who wished to belong in order to give her daughter the opportunity of a good education.[79] Georgianna Bruce, a young English governess, was very much impressed to hear George Ripley, philosopher, gallantly offering to black the boots of one of the men, a simple farmer.[80]

The position of women at Brook Farm was noteworthy. Women had equal property and voting privileges with men and they held high offices in the Association. Sophia Ripley, for example, held two shares of stock and George Ripley's sis-

*Costumes Worn by the Women And Men of the Brook Farm
Community, 1841-1847
Collection of the West Roxbury Historical Society*

ter Marianne Ripley held three. These two women shared with
Charles Anderson Dana, future founder of *The New York Sun*,
the Direction of Education.[81] The common kitchen and nurs-
ery, which Mrs. Ripley had noticed did so much to lighten the
labors of women at Zoar, were used at Brook Farm.

The teachers at Brook Farm seem to have been divided in
their own minds as to how good the school at Brook Farm
really was. Certainly it had an accomplished faculty. George
Ripley taught philosophy and mathematics. Sophia Ripley
taught history and modern languages. Charles Dana taught
German and Greek, and John Sullivan Dwight taught music
and Latin. Abby Morton, who later wrote many popular children's books, was in charge of the Kindergarten. Marianne

Ripley had charge of the younger children. The Transcendentalists were very much interested in the educational theories of Pestalozzi and Rousseau. At Brook Farm the faculty and students mixed together very informally. Studies were elective and included nature study and the learning of farming, gardening and industrial skills. One of the things that caused criticism, in the early period of the school, was the irregularity of the hours.[82] George Bradford thought much time was lost because teachers were busy with farm work and pupils went off into the woods. Sometimes they would fail to make connection at the appointed hours.[83] Even to us now, however, the descriptions of discussions in moral philosophy, the lessons in astronomy under the clear winter sky, the plays and masquerades in the woods, the Dante class in which Charles Dana and Mrs. Ripley and others read Dante in the original without an instructor,[84] the trips into Boston to hear concerts of music by Beethoven, whom John Dwight had taught the Brook Farmers to worship, the singing of Mozart masses, the boat trips on the Charles River make Brook Farm sound like a school to dream about. For any child accustomed to the usual school of the Nineteenth Century it must have been a wonderful experience.[85]

Life at Brook Farm was now a very different thing for Mrs. Ripley than it had been during the summer when she and George lay on green banks listening to the birds singing. Yet besides washing, ironing, scrubbing floors,[86] supervising the running of the house and teaching school, she found time to read and to write for *The Dial.* In January, 1841, she had published an article on "Women."[87] She was impatient of current generalizations:

> All adjusting of the whole sex to a sphere is vain,
> for no two persons naturally have the same. Character, intellect creates the sphere of each.
>
> ...The poet's lovely vision of an ethereal being, hovering half seen above him, in his hour of occupation,

and gliding gently into his retirement…is an exquisite picture for the eye; the sweet verse in which he tells us of her, most witching music to the ear; but she is not woman; she is only the spiritualized image of that tender class of women he loves the best—one whom no true woman could or would become…

…even the clergy have frequently flattered "the feebler sex," by proclaiming to them from the pulpit what lovely beings they may become, if they will only be good, quiet, and gentle, attend exclusively to their domestic duties, and the cultivation of religious feelings, which the other sex very kindly relinquish to them as their inheritance.

This thought that religion is the special prerogative of women seemed to her absurd and dangerous:

…That heaven has placed man and woman in different positions, given them different starting points, (for what is the whole of life, with its varied temporal relationships, but a starting point?) there can be no doubt, but religion belongs to them as beings, not as male and female. The true teacher addresses the same language to both. Christ did so, and this separation is ruinous to the highest improvement of both.

She was especially exasperated by the assumption that women lead a sheltered, contemplative life:

It seems an unknown, or at least an unacknowledged fact, that in the spot where man throws aside his heavy responsibilities his couch of rest is often prepared by his faithful wife, at the sacrifice of all her quiet contemplation and leisure.…She is pursued into her most retired sanctuaries by petty anxieties, haunting her loneliest hour, by temptations taking her by surprise, by cares so harassing, that the most powerful talents and the most abundant intellectual and moral resources are scarce sufficient to give her strength to ward them off. If there is a being exposed to turmoil and indurating care, it is woman, in the retirement of her own home; and if she makes peace and warmth there, it is not by her sweet, religious sensibility, her gentle benevolence, her balmy tenderness, but by a strength and energy as great and untiring as leads man into battle....

Nevertheless Sophia was not pleading for woman's escape from home duties. Quite the reverse:

...If woman's position did not bring out all the faculties of the soul, we might demand a higher for her; but she does not need one higher or wider than nature has given her. Very few of her sex suspect even how noble and beautiful is that which they legitimately occupy, for they are early deprived of the privilege of seeing things as they are.

There follows an attack on the system of educating girls. They should be taught to think for themselves, to "penetrate through externals to principles." They should be encouraged to question the opinions of others and to form their own ideal. Otherwise they lose their own individuality and never gain their husband's respect. Household order and cleanliness must prevail, but they should not be the result of barren drudgery. A girl should be taught to perceive the relationship between household order and the "law which keeps the planets in their course." Finally Sophia outlines her ideal of woman—a serene philosopher, whose own bright spirit outshines prosperity and rises triumphantly above suffering. In conclusion she writes: "Is this the ideal of a perfect woman, and if so, how does it differ from a perfect man?"

Another article for *The Dial* was on "Painting and Sculpture."[88] It is rambling in form. Sophia starts with the thought that a generous nature dislikes to compare things in terms of higher and lower. But she thinks such comparisons one of the necessary limitations of human existence. She prefers, however, to think in terms of means and ends. Her main idea seems to be that sculpture is the culmination of all the other arts. Music, literature and painting portray life in motion. Philosophy and sculpture are the looking back at what has been accomplished, as God contemplated His creation on the day of rest, and the pronouncement, "It is good." Phidias epitomized the civilization of Greece. The sculptor who will do for our more complicated world what Phidias did for Greece has not yet appeared.

Two other thoughts that appear in this article are interesting in view of the social ideal that the Ripleys were trying to work out at Brook Farm. One was a reference to the Scriptural injunction, "let him that is greatest among you be as a servant." The other was in a digression with which Sophia ended her essay:

> I have been watching the flight of birds over a meadow near me, not as an augur, but as a lover of nature. A certain decorousness, and precision, about their delicate course, has for the first time, struck my eye. They are free and bold—but not alone free and bold. Perhaps perfect freedom for man would have the same result, if he grew up in it, and did not ruffle his plumage by contending for it. If it were his unalienable birthright, and not his hard-earned acquisition, would he not wear it gracefully, gently, reservedly? Poor human being, all education is adjusting fetters to thy delicate limbs, and all true manhood is the strife to burst them; happy art thou, if aught remains to thee but strength!

The Brook Farmers were trying their hardest to win "perfect freedom" for man—the freedom of highest self-development combined with the freedom of graceful, willing and loving service.

V

Brook Farm: Trying to Idealize the Actual

It is interesting to compare different Brook Farmers' impressions of Sophia Ripley. Amelia Russell, who was a devoted friend of hers, says: "It is impossible to give an idea of the life she infused into all around her. To talk with her gave us strength for any effort, for 'Impossible' seemed a word unknown to her."[89] She describes how Sophia made the laundry a center of wit and laughter, and often of high philosophic speculation—where Amelia admits she sometimes found herself beyond her depth. Amelia herself, though the Brook Farm expert at clear starching, was pronounced incompetent as a laundress after one trial. But she says she and Sophia Ripley often worked eight and ten hours at a stretch at the ironing boards. She remarks on Sophia's uncompromising obedience to her conscience and relates how she took upon herself the care of little Lucas, a Filipino boy at the school, who had a horrible skin disease. "Mrs. R- performed all the duties of a nurse, and cleaned and bound up the leprous spots without ever betraying to him the sickening feeling which more than once nearly overcame her. By her efforts the disease was arrested for a time, and for more than three years he enjoyed his life with us…"[90]

The Hive, Brook Farm
Collection of the West Roxbury Historical Society

There is a touching legend that Sophia's work in the laundry caused her fingers to bleed until they had to be bandaged. The only evidence I have been able to find for this is the "hearsay" story repeated by Sophia's niece, Isabella, many years later.[91] So many unreliable hearsay stories have grown up about Brook Farm that I certainly would not accept the story as proved. I am happy to report that the Brook Farmers later invented or obtained a washing machine, and some of the men gallantly turned the crank that worked it.

The member of Brook Farm who seems to have felt least in sympathy with Mrs. Ripley was Georgianna Bruce, a young English governess. She concedes Mrs. Ripley's strength of character, but found her uninspiring as a teacher[92] and lacking in motherly understanding of the storms of adolescence.[93] Georgianna recounts that one day when she was helping Mrs. Ripley in the sewing room, she remarked on the affinity which existed between many of the young people. Mrs. Ripley said with some impatience that she was sick of the very word "affinity" and tired of the extravagant moods of the young girls. Just then Mr. Ripley came in and his wife told him with pleasure that a young friend from Boston would be coming to the Farm for a visit. "It will be such a relief, for she doesn't understand the meaning of the word 'idea,' and she has perfectly conventional manners." Poor Georgianna was very much taken aback.[94]

Mary Ann Dwight, the sister of John Sullivan Dwight, tells how gracious Mrs. Ripley was to her on her arrival at Brook Farm. She ran up to her (Mary Ann speaks often of Mrs. Ripley "running," which is not surprising considering what she accomplished) and joked, then told her not to get up to breakfast next morning, but rest a few days, "for if we once began to work, we should never think we could stop."[95] Later on, however, Mary Ann sometimes spoke in less friendly wise. Toward the end of Brook Farm's life, Mary Ann and some friends had thought up a scheme to save the Farm. She remarks "I hear Mr. Ripley is rather pleased—now if it will only please her ladyship."[96] Perhaps, after all, there was something of President Willard in his granddaughter.

Margaret Fuller, who was not a Brook Farmer, though she occasionally visited the Farm, wrote a letter to William Henry Channing in which she spoke of Sophia Ripley as follows:

> Sophia R. read me her letter to you. I told her the truth that I cannot understand her mental processes, and that what she says sounds to me factitious at first, though my confidence in her always prevents my indulging such a thought. I understand her husband much better, though we are so utterly dissimilar, and she usually goes higher and sees clearer than he does. I can talk with him endlessly though not deeply, with her I can go only a step though she loves me and I her, she seldom misunderstands me...[97]

Isaac Hecker spoke of Sophia as " a highly intellectual woman who concealed under a habitual reserve the most elevated sentiments and deepest affections."[98]

The Margaret Fuller Cottage, Brook Farm
Collection of the West Roxbury Historical Society

Perhaps this "reserve" was part of the reason why some persons found Mrs. Ripley unsympathetic. Perhaps in part it was her aesthetic sensitivity, which may have caused her to feel a distaste for some of the people whom her conscience told her she ought to love. I suspect also that she threw herself so passionately into the things she believed in—and her ideals were so high—that she had too little patience and tolerance for others whose thoughts seemed to her to be on a lower level. The following very important letter to Emerson suggests the suffering that this kind of idealism brings with it.

> Brook Farm, July [1843]
>
> …You can hardly know how, like a blessing, such vigorous pages the last issue of the Dial come to one sitting in solitude with the damps and shadows of eveg gathering around the heart at noon day. When we are powerless it is cheering to feel that the age is strong in a few true men & women who can do this age's work & prophesy of the next.

I will tell you how much, not now alone, but always, I feel the want of those around me here who can do the age's work a want more keenly felt by me than it would be by one who took a stand point of more divine serenity, but still a real want. We have "great wealth of nature" here as you truly said, &, if I mistake not a free and vigorous atmosphere for it to unfold in, but I daily & hourly mourn—unwise as it is ever to mourn, at the prodigality with which it is wasted away. I see everywhere around me those who might prophesy of the next age to the present, of eternity to time, prophesying only of themselves, casting their own horoscopes, impertinently prying into their own emotions, or intoxicating themselves with the excited emotions of others; feeling the rising & falling of their own pulse, perhaps recounting its variations to the nearest friend. The lives of our best people here, as elsewhere, are narrow & dreamy, or over-heated. Clear crystal springwater is not their drink, but sweetened, diluted beverage, perhaps spiced wines. And yet if they are born to prophesy will they not in God's own time?

Then though, faithful, like the servant, to their allotted task of the hour, how do they reject the human side of life, turning their back upon the world's work, even when they believe it must be done, & ennobling it not by the seer's eye & prophet's touch, casting their cares upon the merely practical men & women of society—even to the elevating them to a height they have no title to fill even that of rulers in all the external on-goings of life. The movement of many here through the hours & days emits no fragrance, kind hearted as they are, so wrapped up and swathed in selfism are they while the narrow garret of the solitary student is filled with sweetest odours breathing out of every crack & cranny upon the passers by, if he but pursue his lonely thought unconsciously in single-hearted self-forgetfulness. What joy I feel that in the small circle of your nearest friends the craving heart may find such scholars & such workers as we need. So rounded, so strong, so self-sub-sisting. Did you not like our Cousin C. A. D.'s[99] son-net—addressed to all true heroes? It was an organ tone though a monotone. His life is deep-toned too, though not wide. The other Brook Farm poem was very grace-ful, a specimen of the best our young men can now pro-duce, while they refuse themselves to deep experience, & in place thereof indulge in sentiment. Is this only a stage with the best, or must we open our broad acres to a new race, before we see them wrought & trod by men? The ground plan & foundation of our structure suits me well. Many traits in the characters of the builders, or those who with folded arms only look on, I look at quite reverently—almost enviously. It has been good for me, & is still so to be here. I think life could furnish me with nothing better therefore I am content, & ought not to lament if a fair & finished edifice never rises here, but I do not despair even yet. Some might ask, you will not, why I have intruded upon you with this letter. I can only say, just now it was not & now it is written, & after vainly looking for a man or woman where I have most hoped to find them, can I err when I hail some one who appears to me such on the horizon.

Since writing the last lines I have had the pleasure of seeing some true men & women among *our shaker brethren*, vigorous in spiritual life, definite in their aims—robust & equal in practice. Do you know any-thing of them? One of the women—a saint & prophetess might have sat for a picture of Eloise in middle life…[100]

Harsh? Perhaps so—considering that these men and women of Brook Farm were enduring crowded conditions, scant diet and overwork for the sake of their ideal. Yet when we read of the solemnity with which they listened to their characters being "read" by means of holding a letter to the forehead of the "reader," the health fads in which they indulged, the self-conscious cult of their own egos, it is quite possible I think to understand Sophia's impatience.

Another letter to Emerson written later in the same month reiterates her distaste for "sentimentality." It is interesting to notice that Sophia consistently uses the word sentimentality in the sense which William James was to give it later—the indulgence of the feelings without following through into appropriate action. And like James she notes that it is enervating. This second letter also is important for the shift in emphasis it shows in her attitude toward socialism. In her article on Zoar she seemed to be interested primarily in the social effects of collectivization. But increasingly her emphasis will be on the growth of the individual. Socialism is important only as a means to that end:

> …you can hardly realize, how unimportant the results
> of our undertaking, or any undertaking seem to me,
> except that of leading the noblest life. As removing
> some of the external obstacles to such a life, for myself
> & others, I chiefly value our scheme, & gratefully
> accept cooperation; but it is not as cooperators, but as
> men & women that I look on our friends, & demand
> no more of them for being here; only hoping that a
> healthier atmosphere may furnish a better chance for
> vigorous growth. I do not wish or need stronger per-
> sons about me here than elsewhere, & am grateful for
> all the ornamental groups or solitary figures reposing
> in the shade at noon—or gazing on the setting sun;
> but why do they not with clear strong vision meet his
> meridian glance & challenge him as a co-worker to
> run his race with them? Why not live & move with
> head erect under the ardour of his rays, instead of

waiting for the reflection of the last upon some flower or lake? This worship of beauty & increasing life-search for it—is it not, after all only living on the out-skirts of truth. Beauty & truth we are sometimes told are one; but my increasing conviction is that beauty is the attitude of truth, but not truth itself; that we may gaze on it forever, but it will not take us to the cen-tre—& that its pursuit & study are enervating, crush-ing some of our strongest spirits. Let us live truly, & we shall be beautiful, for in this sense truth & beauty are one.[101]

The letter closes with a reference to a recent loss. This was probably the death of her little nephew Franky Dana, whose sixth birthday had been celebrated by a fancy dress party in the woods of Brook Farm, recounted in Hawthorne's *American Notebooks*.[102] Sophia had been very devoted to the little boy. In her letter to John Sullivan Dwight in February 1840 she had written, "Little Franky was not so much out of the way when he said 'Aunt Sophia can't I get up to heaven on the snowflakes when they are falling.'"[103] He died in May 1843. The loss may help to account for the depression which drove Sophia to sit down and write to Emerson. It also seems to have set her pondering the question of the immortality of the soul. To many of the Transcendentalists, including Emerson, immortality meant that one is part of God *now*, and when one's own personal existence is over, God lives yet. Sophia wrote rather forlornly:

> …The sense of my loss, except at intervals, is less live-ly than it was—& seems to have occurred centuries ago; this is very saddening to me. It produces a dead-ness of feeling that makes everything in life seem very far off to me, not so unreal as before, but more unin-teresting. Still if life, this life is precious—if every moment is as opulent as just now it seemed to me—it will assert itself again & reclaim its own. Meanwhile I

wait. And yet how mean that the sense of present immortality—*that I am immortal now*, is not enough to carry me through life with unfaltering step.

In the fall of 1843 Brook Farm enlarged its membership to take in mechanics and tradesmen, shoemakers, carpenters, etc. (Were these perhaps to be Sophia's "new race?") The purpose was to make the Farm as self-subsisting and complete as possible. Some of the members felt later that it was a mistake to divert talent and attention away from the school into these new fields. Another difficulty was that the enlargement brought in men and women less congenial to the intellectual and refined Transcendentalists than most of the earlier members. Some of the original members left soon after.

To the Ripleys it was a matter of principle, aside from practical considerations, if they were going to "renew the face of the earth," to take in all classes of men. But they came to feel that a unifying purpose was necessary to weld together the diverse groups. In an undated letter to Margaret Fuller Sophia Ripley wrote:

> ...The money does not come. We have meetings every week at which the men out of the Association are present. They are called on to help us, & are full of spirit & good sense in their suggestions. They are very united, & are attempting to make an arrangement by which our mechanical departments may be increased, & the support of the establishment thrown in a great measure upon them. Our faith increases, even when hope is faint, & love abounds. I suffer very much from George's perplexities (entre nous) because I can not aid him in them, & one does not feel that right to rise above the trials of others, into a clearer & serener atmosphere, where our own trials of every kind can often lift us.[104]

In another letter dated simply "Thursday," she wrote again,

discussing some recent unpleasant misunderstandings:

> I received yesterday your letter of sweet affectionate
> sympathy & enquiry, & it came just at the moment
> when I was feeling as if I should be very glad to see you
> or write to you, & quickens me to do the last as I can-
> not accomplish the first. I am glad to see that my keep-
> ing back part of what was in my mind the Sunday we
> talked together did not strike you as disingenuous (as it
> really was not) but seems not to have made any impres-
> sion. I had not made up my mind in what manner to
> communicate to George the revelations of the week, &
> until he knew them, I could not mention them to any-
> one else; at the same time they had really lost the
> importance in my view which they had temporarily
> assumed. The heart was not deeply wounded, for it had
> never been deeply attached to the persons concerned,
> & my intellect obtained one clear result, to aid in future
> action; that where the tender ties of affinity of nature
> do not draw one, the only legitimate union is found in
> oneness of purpose which in all but extreme cases,
> secure good faith. This oneness of purpose, involving
> of course much kind consideration & tolerance is the
> closest tie which can bind us to the majority of men, &
> the conscience, which demands some sort of tie, is sat-
> isfied thereby. This union I at present believe I find in
> Association, & to Association I purpose to devote my
> life; all relations but the nearest, seem quite small &
> secondary, in presence of this purpose, except so far as
> they throw light on its practical workings. Our meet-
> ing, confined to a few, had some very good points, but
> was not satisfactory on the whole. It did nothing
> towards renewing the tie that had been ruptured, so far
> as we were concerned; though the opposite parties pro-
> fessed to be perfectly satisfied with the explanations
> made where there was no fault, & *involved* in frank con-

fessions of error where it had been committed, however unconsciously. All nobleness was on the part of the injured, (George,[105] Charles[106] & Georgie[107])—I detected it no where else, though there was much kindness & good-nature, & many of those truthful things said, that I never heard anywhere but here. I am convinced there would have been no manly calling to account of any of us, if Georgy's truthfulness, had not forced persons into it. There was great care taken to say nothing untrue, but equal care not to commit any persons who had broken good faith, by telling the whole truth & frankly confessing want of generosity. I could detect no-where any, the faintest intellectual perception of the violation of the law of right—nowhere, regret for irreparable injury nowhere those delicate perceptions of the nature of others & the subtle relations between human souls, which we have no reason to expect, after all, except from fine natures or natures made fine by culture. Character is pretty well understood here, actions of course too, but natures, particularly reserved & delicate ones not at all, & much that you would esteem a necessary & pleasing manifestation of a superior nature, is set down to the account of faults. But patience!—All men will be here represented in due time—the finest last, meanwhile there are many true as steel. Georgie has been true to herself—& through much rashness, & some ignorance has worked her way into justice & nobleness, as she always will.

I am sorry for Charles' partial failure, which he was aware of himself; though I love in him that which caused it. When he left here he was in a state above all personality, & self consciousness, & could he have spoken then, or sustained his elevation he would have done nobly. I am deeply interested in all measures, pursuing, or to be pursued in regard to our future & demand that they should be vigorous, but still I cannot feel very solicitous or very sad about the future. We have been led & shall be led & I feel more & more that in these days we must take our life in our own hands, be ready to dwell no where, to encamp any where, & give to our work that devoted loyal love, which we have hitherto given to our localities, friends & environments. George is suffering from these things more than I am. He has less varied ties than I to persons & things about him, & when his one link is broken he feels it deeply, then unpleasant associations come up which he finds it hard to get over. Still he is nobly supported here by two or three & I trust will be carried through. His heart warms to Association on a great scale, & here I warmly unite to him.....I am more delicate I think than usual, but take good care. Mr. Bradford encourages me to begin Homer in the original, & this is a cordial — [108]

The type of "Association" that the Brook Farmers determined to adopt was Fourierism. According to Fourier, God has so designed the world that "attractions are in proportion to destinies." The kind of labor a man is attracted toward is the kind God created him to perform. Moreover, since God is all wise, there are exactly enough men in the world of the right kind for each kind of labor. Social ills are the result of men failing to realize God's benevolent plan for man. The history of the world is divided into periods advancing from barbarism through "civilization" (which had very unsavory implications of cut-throat competition) to ultimate "harmony." When men conform their society to *God's own* social laws, heaven will reign on earth.

At first sight it might seem strange that Transcendentalists would adopt so *mechanical* an explanation of good and evil. On the other hand, since Transcendentalists believed that men are essentially good, the explanation of evil as simply the result of faulty external conditions must have appealed to them as humane and charitable. Moreover, the Brook Farmers found in Fourier's doctrines a powerful challenge to try to create conditions which would enable the individual to achieve the maximum of self-fulfillment. Unfortunately we have no complete exposition of Sophia Ripley's ideas about Fourier. She seems to have been strongly attracted, though with some reservations. I have quoted her letter to Margaret Fuller. Georgianna Bruce quotes a letter from her:

> I am greatly drawn of late to a close study of Fourier. His science of association recommends itself more and more to my feelings and conscience, and I am constrained to accept him as a man of genius, a discoverer; though I believe that in many things his system is to be modified by the spirit of our time and nation. The unfolding of the groups and series is as beautiful to me as the opening of the buds and leaves in spring, and will give a grace and charm to the actual never imagined before.[109]

In 1845 the Brook Farm Association was incorporated as the Brook Farm Phalanx. Its new constitution[110] provided that industries should be organized in groups, which should elect leaders every week. These groups were small and engaged in one particular job, e.g., milking. The groups were arranged in series, whose leaders were elected every two months. The government of the Phalanx as a whole was invested in a General Council, consisting of four branches, Industry, Finance, Science, and the President. For ordinary purposes of administration, the President and chairmen of each branch acted as a special council. An advisory council, known as the Areopagus, consisted of the General Council as well as the chiefs of the groups and series. The General Council appointed a Council of Arbiters to listen to complaints and grievances and settle questions of morals and manners. This Council of Arbiters was to consist of seven members, *a majority of whom must be women*! It was hoped that the central government would provide Unity of purpose, while the self-government within the groups and

Brook Farm Money, signed by Charles A. Dana
Collection of the West Roxbury Historical Society

series would provide Energy in operation. The Phalanx's guarantees to its members and its principles regarding distribution of profits were so interesting and grappled so effectively with problems facing us today, that I quote them:

> The Capital stock of the Phalanx shall be divided into three classes: first, Loan Stock, or that which receives a fixed interest of five per cent per annum; second, Partnership Stock, or that whose dividend depends upon the general product of the Phalanx; third, Labor Stock, or that which represents the dividend to Labor…
>
> **Guarantees.** The Phalanx guarantees suitable employment to all its members, to each according to his tastes, talents, and acquirements, to the end that both the community and the individual may derive the greatest benefit from the services of every person. It also guarantees the means of subsistence, and in sickness or old age furnishes ample support, medical attendance, and all requisite care, without any charge whatever, except in case of those who have the means of paying such expenses. Education is guaranteed with-

out charge to all, both to members and their children. Means of the highest culture are freely opened to all.

Organization of Labor. It is also provided that Labor shall be distinguished according to its character as necessary, useful, or attractive; its use in the promotion of the harmony of society is also regarded.

Division of Profits. Its great feature...is the reconciliation of the various interests of society which it effects. And in the very particular which economists and learned men of all sorts have given up in despair, namely, the relations of capital and labor, the union is most complete. The old and deep rooted conflict between these two great social powers, a conflict which produces at this moment more misery in the world than any other cause whatever, is altogether removed by the simple and efficacious method of Association.

The dividend to Labor is to be so distributed that the class of labors which in ordinary society are generally worse paid, and are more disreputable than others, on account of their disagreeableness, shall receive the highest reward, while those which are more attractive and afford a certain compensation in the pleasure of their performance receive the lowest reward,—an arrangement by which only justice is done, though the methods of civilized society are in it altogether reversed.[111]

The practical details of the scheme were sometimes extremely complicated—for instance the book keeping for those who changed often from one type of occupation to another, which was necessary to replace the sick or disabled, and indeed was an integral part of the system. For too long a time at one job was considered "unattractive." In the early days of Brook Farm people had simply pitched in informally where they seemed to be needed. Now it was necessary to

THE HARBINGER,

DEVOTED TO SOCIAL AND POLITICAL PROGRESS.

ALL THINGS, AT THE PRESENT DAY, STAND PROVIDED AND PREPARED, AND AWAIT THE LIGHT.

BURGESS, STRINGER, AND COMPANY, No. 222 Broadway, New York.	PUBLISHED BY THE BROOK FARM PHALANX.	REDDING AND COMPANY, No. 8 State Street, Boston.
VOLUME II.	SATURDAY, DECEMBER 27, 1845.	NUMBER 3.

MISCELLANY.

COSMOGONY.

FROM A MANUSCRIPT OF FOURIER.
Translated for the Harbinger.

CHAPTER II. (*Continued.*)

I have sufficiently shown that a creation is the concurrent work of all the planets, in which each one intervenes according to its qualities; the details I will give hereafter. I will show by what method we discern the work of each. Till then, if we ask of the civilizees: Who created cabbages! Who created plums! they ought to answer: We know nothing at all about it. We are ignorant of the laws of Aromal movement, of the origin and distribution of the primitive germs. They should beware of answering: It was God who created the plums! The satellites of Herschel, each one modelling according to its dominant passion.

I will not stop to give an aromal catechism after this fashion, which would lead us too far, since the vegetable kingdom alone would furnish thirty thousand questions of origin, and a thousand times more, thirty millions of questions, about the properties and modifications of each vegetable species. What would it be with the other kingdoms! Each of these questions demands studies, researches, upon which I have often run aground after long labor, although I possess the key to this science. I have in vain sought what star has made us a present of the toad; my suspicions rest upon Mars. I have all along limited myself to some few of the most remarkable problems, which will suffice to put naturalists and competent persons upon the track, The questions of causes will turn first upon the general plan adopted before creating plums and all the other products which are the work of the different satellites of Herschel. How did they class the characters and functions of Love, represented allegorically by the Apricots and Plums! how did they distribute the different parts among the ten planets of the Scale of Love! how regulate the competency of each to represent such a table of the effects of Love! Why was it ordained that the fruit of Hebe should be green sprinkled with white! that the fruit of Cleopatra should be yellow, touched with a purple spot! How may we be assured that these arrangements were the regular emblems of such a species of Love! Finally, what were the discussions and calculations after which they resolved upon the forms, colors, tastes, and good or bad properties to be distribut-

Part of a Page from "The Harbinger," with an Article by Charles Fourier
From Original in the Boston Public Library

Part of a page from The Harbinger
From original in the Boston Public Library

keep track of how many hours one spent in each group. And according to Amelia Russell, there grew up a kind of etiquette between groups. She tells a ludicrous story:

> A neighbor once coming to visit us met one of the members rushing wildly about the place, and asked him what was the matter, thinking some great calamity must have occurred. "Oh! the pigs have got into the cornfield, and I am looking for the Miscellaneous Group to drive them out." He himself could not think of interfering with the rights of others.[112]

Besides farming, industries and the school, the Brook Farmers edited the Associanist newspaper *The Harbinger*. Mrs. Ripley seems to have written for it sometimes and to have helped in editorial work. Since she invariably worked anonymously it is difficult to know how much she did. In a letter to Charlotte Dana, September, 1846, she wrote: "*The Harbinger* is like a precious child to me..."[113] and in the following year she wrote to Longfellow from New York: "As soon as I am quietly settled, I hope to prepare for *The Harbinger* a short notice of the distinguished men of Cuba with extracts from 'Las Flores del Siglo.' How much I wish I could be near you that you might teach me the best way of doing such things!"[114]

In 1845 the Brook Farmers started the building of a "Phalanstery" to accommodate their increased membership in decent comfort and allow for taking in new members. The members had been astonishingly self-sacrificing in the matter of living quarters, being packed in like sardines and shifted about frequently between the several houses. Now, in the fall of 1845 they were looking forward with pleasure to this new building. It was to have little apartments for families, where they could enjoy their privacy and eat either by themselves or in the general dining room as they preferred. It was also to have a chapel. There seems to have been an enthusiastic interest in religion at this period on the part of some of the members under the leadership of William Henry Channing. One of their favorite rites was to join hands in a circle symbolic of Universal Unity—of men with man, with Nature and with God. Mrs. Ripley is said to have been interested in the movement.[115] But the practice of religion was completely optional at Brook Farm and many varieties of opinion were represented. The chapel was not to be considered sectarian.

In March 1846, the day the workmen started afresh on the new building after the winter's respite, the Phalanstery caught fire and burned to the ground. The Brook Farmers were helpless to prevent it. George Ripley bore up with remarkable courage, and when the firemen arrived—too late—offered them refreshments with the remark, "Had we but known, or even suspected you were coming, we would have been better prepared to receive you and given you a worthier, if not a warmer reception!"[116]

Sophia Ripley is said to have turned away and been unable to look at the fire.[117] Brook Farm's finances had always been precarious. The Ripleys seem to have chosen the site for its beauty without enquiring too carefully about its fertility. Even

Tragic History of Fire at Brook Farm
(The Phalanstery fire was in 1846, later fires in 1973 and 1985)
Collection of the West Roxbury Historical Society

their devoted friend Amelia Russell could not refrain from saying:

> I have not ventured to speak of the capabilities of the place with respect to cultivation, for being a woman I am not supposed to know much about its working details; but having lived for the greater part of my life in the country, I think I know somewhat of the quality of land when I see it, and I do not think much of that possessed by Brook Farm was suited to arable purposes. It is not for me to criticize the knowledge of those so infinitely my superiors, but I cannot say that gravel and sand, interspersed with picturesque rocks, produce very rich grass.[118]

Since Brook Farm had become a Phalanx many people had been hesitant about sending their children to the school, for fear they would learn dangerous ideas. Fourier had done some speculating about the state of marriage in the ultimate perfect society, suggesting that some persons were perhaps unsuited to permanent matches. The Brook Farmers reiterated that these speculations had nothing to do with their experiment and that they had highest reverence for the marriage bond and the sanctity of the family. Nevertheless their school suffered from these ideas of Fourier's, so there was another source of income weakened. In 1845 Hawthorne, whose finances were as straitened as the Ripleys, had sued Ripley and Charles A. Dana for money advanced by him.[119] Sophia had seen George carrying the burden of worry and suffered for him. Now here was the Phalanstery for which they had borrowed $30,000 going up in smoke. And it had not yet been insured!

A few days later Sophia wrote John Sullivan Dwight, who was in New York lecturing to raise money and persuading the creditors to forego interest on their loans, that the General Council was considering selling the property and starting anew.[120] But later it was decided to try to keep on with Brook Farm, cutting out most of the industries and depending on the School and *The Harbinger* for support. Mary Ann Dwight wrote to a friend that the Ripleys and her own brother wanted to hire out the farm. She felt they were giving up their principles in so doing. She and her husband-to-be, John Orvis, suggested that the farm and some of the industries be kept on an associative basis, while those who were running the school pay board for themselves and the scholars to the association. This might have been a good idea. Mary Ann said: "I hear Mrs. Ripley is rather pleased."[121]

Unfortunately members of Brook Farm gradually began to leave for opportunities elsewhere. The financial panic of 1837 had given way to recovery. So some of the economic motives causing individuals to try socialistic experiments were gone. When profits and pay were attractive enough in private industry, the attractions of Association seemed to decrease.

For a year and a half longer the Ripleys and some friends

kept on. They threw themselves into making the school the best they possibly could. Sophia Ripley had been ill for a time after the fire, according to Mary Ann Dwight.[122] But by summer she was more buoyant than ever. On September 12th she was writing:

> What glorious summer weather we have had, particularly the last two or three weeks. I cannot describe to you the joy of my physical existence those hottest days. It seemed to me I had a glimpse of that angelic state where the body is glorified, & the soul aided & supported by it in its highest action. I trod on air, my brain was clear, my spirit serene. No amount of labor was too great for me, four or five hours sleep was all I required. I rose at $4^{1}/_{2}$ & went through the woods & across the fields, a most lovely walk, to the river with the girls; & there we were in the river waiting the sunrise. All the long evegs were spent in the woods or walking in the garden, & the golden, brilliant light of the moon that turned night into day, put to shame all the recently announced theories of the ruined condition of that planet.

"I have some fine boys with me now, & my school is delightful."[123] But still the membership kept falling off. Finally on October 20, 1847, Mrs. Ripley wrote to Longfellow:

> I had hoped that during the fine weather of the last few days you would have found leisure for a drive to Brook Farm, & I particularly regret that we have not had the pleasure of seeing you there as we have this week left it, for our new home in New York.[124]

George Ripley shouldered the debts remaining after the sale of Brook Farm. It took the rest of Sophia's lifetime for the Ripleys to discharge this burden. George made the last payment in the shape of a set of the *Cyclopedia Americana* in 1862, almost two years after Sophia's death.[125]

VI
Conversion to Catholicism

In her letters to Emerson in 1843 Sophia Ripley had expressed a sense of the emptiness of Transcendentalism and of the futility of the "life search for beauty." Truth was at the core of things, beauty only the periphery. She was seeking for Truth, and for a definite aim for life.[126] This longing seems to have increased. For a time she hoped to find the aim in Association. But Association could only make "external arrangements." Still the longing was within. For a time she was an eager follower of William Henry Channing. But some time between October 1845 and September 1846 she became seriously interested in Catholicism. In her letter to Charlotte Dana of September 1, 1846—the same letter in which she wrote of her physical exaltation and her early mornings dips in the river with the school girls—she wrote:

> …I have some fine boys with me now, & my school is delightful. Most reverently did I consecrate it at its opening at New Year to our blessed mother & need I tell you how tenderly she has guarded it over since. Thank you for the little stamp. I wear it constantly as a talisman. On Friday I was in town & could as well

as not have heard Bishop Hughes funeral sermon & attended high Mass—but did not know of it till too late.[127]

Charlotte Dana and another intimate friend, Julia Metcalf, had been received recently into the Catholic Church. So Sophia added:

> Horace[128] says he did not express to Julia and yourself half the sympathy he felt, because there is so much sentimentalism now a days about Catholicism that he thought you would not know that it was a deeper feeling with him.
>
> Can I describe to you my horror when the 1st of Sept came & I found your Autumn breviary in my drawer? I hope you have recd it safely long since. Do send me a good book to read—I am hungering & thirsting. I want to send you some translations from French associative papers in late numbers of the Harbinger, showing the position of our Phalansterian friends to the Catholic Church. Will you read them? The Harbinger is like a precious child to me, & I would not see it used for curl papers or lamp-lighters except to light a torch before the Image of our Holy Mother. George has lent me too a remarkable letter from Mr. Brownson[129] to him, to show to you.

The following May Sophia wrote again to Charlotte:

> …I never enjoyed our Church so much as yesterday. I seemed to partake more largely of the depths of its richness, & I truly longed to follow the little band, *without saying a word or being asked a question*, who had the privilege of partaking of the blessed sacrament. I hope before a great while I may have the chance of seeing some Catholic who has been long eno' in the Church to answer all my questions.[130]

By September she seems to have made up her mind that she wanted to become a Catholic. She wrote:

Brook Farm Friday Sept 3d 1847

Dearest Charlotte

I can hardly believe that ten days have passed since we parted, & I have not written to you yet. I have been very much engaged with teaching & company, & then you are so near me always that I have to withdraw myself from you to write. Julie has by this time written to you, or *told* you of our pleasant Sunday. I accepted the cross of going with the person of my acquaintance who has always had in the greatest degree that mixture of hatred & contempt for the Catholic church, so common among Protestants. A person of the coolest, keenest & most subtle intellect, & one who out Emersoned Emerson, in his skepticism.[131] He for the first time, on this visit, spoke respectfully of the church; so much so, that I was able to tell him all that was in my soul about it, which could be spoken out; for he has spiritual tendencies, & many other fine traits which have always bound me to him. I could hardly believe my senses when I actually found him there. He says he was deeply impressed by the service, & bore with the meekness of a child Father O'Brien's public reproof of his unholy use of his opera glass— he—who is more keenly alive to reproof than any one I know. He warns me however against going any farther than merely indulging my sentiments by attending church, talks of the charm being broken if I should enter it etc—All of which proved to me how little one can penetrate into the condition of another merely by intellectual perceptions however acute they may be. John Cheever[132] feels my position a thousandfold more truly. Another of our associative family (an ex universalist minister is to be received shortly).[133]

She goes on to speak of Frank Shaw, neighbor and bene-
factor of Brook Farm, and of his brother Coolidge, who had
become a Catholic and who later joined a religious order:

> My friend Frank Shaw came to see me one eveg this
> week. He has been talking constantly with his brother
> ever since he has been in this country about the church,
> & he tells me that the result has been to drive him fur-
> ther from it than ever; yet he attends it constantly &
> can get satisfaction from no other. Why will people talk
> so much—instead of kneeling with folded hands, to
> receive whatever divine grace may be bestowed on
> them. Frank does not regard the sentiments as the
> legitimate vehicle for the descent of the Spirit & the
> atmosphere thro' which truth is most clearly revealed.
> He uses his reason solely, in questioning Coolidge. The
> latter cannot reason about his faith, & is too much a
> Shaw to excite the sentiments of his brother, he simply
> says *"I believe"* & this is not enough for F-.

She must have taken the final step the end of 1847 or the
beginning of 1848.[134] For on January 23 1848 she wrote
Longfellow about his poem *Evangeline*:

> Flatbush, L.I.
> Sunday eveg Jan 23d 1847 sic
>
> My dear Sir
>
> Amid the floods of praise that have been pouring in
> upon you since the publication of your Evangeline it
> would seem almost superfluous for a retired individ-
> ual to add their pittance of applause; but fresh from
> the first reading of it, for the fitting time never came
> to me till now, I cannot bring myself to lay my head
> upon my pillow till I have told you how much more
> beautiful the world seems to me for containing such
> an exquisite creation. As the pious Catholic with taper
> & holy water in hand consecrates the domain which

he has appropriated to himself for a home, so have you consecrated the soil of your country, from the pine forests of the East to the prairies of the West.

We have to thank you too for the effort it must have cost you to commit this delicate child of your soul, who must have grown up in a retirement more sacred than any you had before known, to the world with its coarse criticism, & still coarser praises; May she never be sullied by either. You will forgive it to the fanaticism of a newly received child of the church, if I say that the tribute of devotion you have offered to this our Holy Mother, by the expression of your Catholic sympathies seems to me to have been repaid to you by a deeper inspiration than your Muse had ever before received

with grateful respect

Yrs

Sophia W. Ripley[135]

How did it happen that Sophia Ripley turned to Catholicism for her solution? For one thing William Henry Channing himself was attracted to the Catholic Church. In the first two issues of *The Dial* he had written a story, "Ernest the Seeker," about two young men, one of whom went to Rome and became a priest. The other (Ernest) was strongly attracted aesthetically but finally rejected Catholicism for the sake of his intellectual liberty.[136] It seems quite likely that the story was a projection of an internal struggle of Channing's own. He had thought of becoming a Catholic while a young man in Rome and had been dissuaded by his uncle, William Ellery Channing.[137]

Then, too, there was quite a widespread interest in things Catholic among Romanticists, both in Europe and America. At Brook Farm the members sang Masses and oratorios, and many of them read Dante, St. Augustine and Pascal. As in Europe the growing willingness to study things Catholic led in some cases to conversion. Orestes Brownson, a close friend of

George Ripley's, and Isaac Hecker, who acted as baker at Brook Farm and later was a visitor, were both received into the Church in 1844. That summer Isaac Hecker visited Brook Farm and told of his experience. He said later that Mrs. Ripley showed keen interest in what he had to say.[138] Within the next two years, as is shown in the letters quoted above, several other friends of Mrs. Ripley's became Catholics.

Sophia Ripley was undoubtedly attracted aesthetically to Catholicism. But given her conviction on the relationship between truth and beauty, I think she would never have become a Catholic simply for that reason. Her husband would write of Sophia's "singular integrity both of mind and heart."[139] Whatever the aesthetic or emotional appeal of a religion, she would have to be convinced of its *truth*.

Sophia Ripley did not leave an account of what led her to embrace Catholicism. But occasional remarks in her letters can serve as clues. One such remark relates to Calvinism:

> I did not tell you with what a gentle shudder & tone of profound compassion the Bishop spoke in his instructions of the horrible doctrines of original sin and total depravity—so diffused through Protestantism, that even those who have never believed in them feel their withering power.[140]

According to Catholic teaching, man lost by Adam's sin the supernatural gift of union with God, and his intellect was clouded and his will weakened so that he was easily tempted to sin. Nevertheless he still longs for goodness and his intellect tends toward truth. Sophia perhaps found this teaching a good middle of the road position between the "horrible doctrines" of Calvinism and the rosy optimism of the Transcendentalists and Fourierists which, after she had coped with all sorts and kinds of people at Brook Farm, may have seemed unrealistic.

Another remark relates to the pantheistic tendencies in Transcendentalism:

I dreamed that I went into Marianne's room and found her, in the morng, kneeling at a little oratory at her devotions! If I mistake not a rare thing for her. She is a consistent Protestant, and I respect her for not trying to pray, when she has never been taught how, & *the object of her prayers is as vague and unreal as the shadow of a cloud.* But I commiserate most tenderly those whose natures compel them to pray under such circumstances. How much they suffer![141]

Perhaps the best clue to Sophia's line of thought is the book which she chose to translate from the French immediately after her conversion. *Religion in Society, Solution of Great Problems* by the Abbe Martinet.[142] The following letter to Orestes Brownson gives her reasons for translating the book and her high opinion of it. It is also interesting for its account of the relationship between herself and her husband after her conversion. O. B. Frothingham in his biography of George Ripley says that the Ripleys agreed not to discuss questions of religious opinion, and Lindsay Swift speaks of Sophia's religion as the "forbidden ground upon which neither cared to enter."[143] This letter and others would seem to indicate otherwise:

New York Tuesday July 10th 1849

Dear Sir:

As I know your weariness of the pen & utter distaste to answering letters, I am very reluctant to write one which will require an immediate response; but I always had great faith in your Christian kindness, *before you were a Christian*, & have still more confidence in it, since it has been ennobled into Catholic charity....

You took so kind an interest in my translation, "des Grands Problemes," when I first mentioned it to you, that I have always considered it destined to appear before the public under your auspices. I have been industriously at work upon it for some weeks, & must be a sad bungler not to give a pretty good translation, for I have the benefit of Mr. Ripley's verbal criticism of it as I go along, you know how valuable that is, & of Dr. Cummings' verbal & Catholic criticism which is very important. Both Mr. Ripley and Dr. C- consider it best that the two first vols, or the first series, as the author terms it, should be published first, & the second after a reasonable interval. I am now quite ready to go to press....As I go on with the work it assumes increasing importance, & in the present state of Protestantism in this country, has a [sic] great missionary labour to perform. It seems to me calculated to have more effect upon Protestant thinking men and women of the present day than any Catholic book I have ever seen. Though brilliant & witty, it is very earnest & thorough, and leaves no point of Catholic doctrine or morals untouched.

Though the form of the work is popular, it bears the marks on every page, of the most profound thought & patient labour, & an almost supernatural insight into the intellectual habits & tendencies of all classes & conditions of men from rationalistic Germany to rationalistic & ultra transcendental Massachusetts.

I find several Catholics, who know of the book, holding it in the same estimation as myself, though perhaps the rather exaggerated mode of expression with regard to it, allowed to a recent convert, would be tempered in their case by a more Catholic moderation. Mr. Ripley, who tells me that at every step his intellect repudiates the arguments of the writer, acknowledges his statements to be admirably well made. And though regarding the work as full of wretched sophistry is extremely desirous that it should be perfectly well done & "put through" with spirit. He would be happy to aid in any way; but with all his heresies thick about him, there would be no advantage in his appearing in

> the matter, so that I am thrown entirely on the kind-
> ness & courtesy of Catholic friends, upon whom I feel
> the most entire reliance.[144]

What then was this book, which Sophia found so convinc-
ing and George so sophistical? It was an attempt to show that
Catholicism was in harmony with human experience and was
the elevation and fulfillment of the deepest natural longings of
man's mind and heart. It started with the statement that man
is distinguished from the brutes by his possession and use of
reason. Because of his reason he wants to know what he is,
where he comes from and what the purpose of his life is. If he
shrugs off these questions and is indifferent to them, than he is
degrading himself below the brutes. For to live aimlessly for
them is natural, but for man unnatural.

To the question "From whence does man come" the author
says there are four current solutions: indifference, materialism, pantheism, and belief in a personal God. Indifference is
unintelligent. Materialism ignores the principle of unity in
man, and his awareness of himself as a person. It ignores
order in the universe and the nature of life. Pantheism is self-
worship and is moreover destructive of morals, when followed
to its logical conclusions. For the most shocking crimes are
simply self expressions of the Deity. The only true solution is
that God is Necessary Being, who makes all other existence
possible, the source of life, spirit and moral values. He is the
magnet that has drawn men to holiness in all ages.

Man's aspirations are infinite. They cannot be satisfied by
material possessions, which are always limited in time. They
can only be satisfied by union with God, "an unfathomable
and shoreless ocean of goodness, power, and beauty." If we
could contemplate God's essence now, "he would, of course,
take captive our love." Through respect for our liberty he veils
himself from us for a time. According to our choice *for* God or
against him here, we are already turning our souls in the direction they will take for eternity: Heaven, that is union with

God; or Hell, the loss of God and subjection *to our own sins.*

Adam by his sin extinguished the grace of God in his soul. How then could he transmit it to his children? As his will had revolted against God, so his passions revolted against him. How then could he transmit an unfaltering mind and will? The effects of "original sin" are so apparent within ourselves and in the world about us, it is remarkable that the doctrine should ever have been called in question. Christ, the God-Man, made a way for us to regain God's grace, leaving us a Church to strengthen and unite us to himself in the Sacraments. Those who love God, but who are outside the body of the Church, because they have not yet recognized its truth, are joined to it in spirit by baptism of desire.

If it were left to our intellects alone to find the way of salvation, only trained scholars with leisure for thought and study would be able to lead purposive lives. But God wants all, even little children and the poor and ignorant, to do so. Through the divine gift of faith and the teaching of the Church they can. Besides, since God is infinite man's finite reason cannot encompass him. Therefore there was need of revelation.

The remainder of the book is devoted to showing that a vital Christianity would remake the earth. Sickness and suffering would remain to try our mettle, but injustice, hatred and wars would be wiped out and the warmth of Christian charity would transfigure human relationships. Revolutions and redistributions of property can never achieve this end, because the oppressed, once they achieved power, would begin to oppress one another. The only solution is the striving after individual sanctity, with the universal Church to sting the consciences, guide, nourish and unite rich and poor, rulers and governed, throughout the world.

So now at last Sophia felt that she was really pursuing Truth and had found her life's aim. The renewing of the face of the earth was indeed "work for a God." It could only be done in union with him![145]

VII

"Servant of the Servants of God"

or the first year after the Ripleys came to New York they lived in Flatbush, which in those days was "a love-ly, romantic village."[146] George Ripley continued to edit *The Harbinger*. Sophia opened a school.[147] In her spare time she studied her new religion with Bishop Hughes. She also made acquaintance eagerly with Catholics, both clergy and lay, and read voraciously. Her intellect found wonderful fulfillment in these studies. "How rich is the conversation of all these blessed priests. How meagre all the best things we have ever heard, seem in comparison. The whole church speaks through them at every moment,"[148] she wrote to her cousin, after a con-versation with Dr. Jeremiah Williams Cummings, first pastor of St. Stephens Church. And on another occasion she wrote, "How every sweet spiritual flower of thought, that attracts us even in our Protestant reading, faded & wilted as it may be by transplantation there, blooms out fresh & fragrant in its own rich Catholic soil. Oh what born thieves are we Protes-tants!"[149] A few days after Easter in 1848 she wrote, "I am rev-eling in St. Elisabeth's Life."[150] In May again she spoke of this saint: "You know my St. Elisabeth, & how my heart flew to

Josiah Walcott Painting of Brook Farm, ca. 1846. The buildings, from left, are Pilgrim House, The Cottage, The Eyrie (and in front of it the remains of the Phalanstery) and The Hive Collection of the Massachusetts Historical Society

her the first time I heard of her. Will you believe it, she named her first daughter Sophia, and her second daughter Sophia!"[151] A Scotch convert, Father McLellan, introduced her to "the modern French school of Catholic writers." She was particularly interested in "the correspondence between modern geological discoveries, & the mosaic accounts of the creation."[152] In May 1849 she discovered St. Teresa: "I am studying—yes studying—for her life contains the science of prayer in all its depths—the writings of St. Theresa. They came to me just at the right time—when the glories of meditation are slowly opening upon me."[153]

In her eagerness and enthusiasm for her new faith, Sophia, in addition to her more serious studies in theology and mysticism, drank in Catholic folklore and popular devotions. She and George's niece, Sarah Stearns, made friends with all the Catholics in the neighborhood. Of Sarah, Sophia wrote:

> …she has a more Catholic look than any of us, for all the Catholic men, women & children in the streets speak to her, & give her seats in churches, & take her home, & refresh her with cold water, & present her with nice little books of devotion & choice spiritual reading, such as cannot be procured at any price in this country.[154]

Sophia and Sarah also listened respectfully to the instructions of Marianne Ripley's cook.[155] Sophia was "devoured with envy" because Julia Metcalf was sometimes taken for a *"born Catholic!"*[156]

In the Lent of 1848 Sophia went through a kind of spiritual crisis. She was helped in her difficulty by Bishop Hughes:

> …Sunday morng I woke long before light, & my thoughts fastened themselves on a subject, I often mentioned to you when you were here, the coldness of heart in Protestantism, & my own very cold heart in particular. A clear revelation of myself was made to me

as never before, I saw that all through life my ties with others were those of the intellect & imagination, & not warm human heart ties; that I do not love anyone and never did, with the heart, & of course never could have been worthy in any relation. Every part of my life was more clearly explained to me than ever before, & I saw what had caused my greatest difficulties & trials. I saw above all that my faith in the church was only a reunion of my intellect with God; that in the region of intellect it was growing clearer & firmer every day; that it filled my imagination completely, & that these fluttering restless joys, that I experience in common with many other converts from Protestantism, were from a gratified imagination & not a sanctified heart — I saw that faith requires to strike root in the heart, & if the stony soil refuses to receive it, it has nowhere to plant itself & therefore has no root at all. I saw how, all through my life I had been trying to do good to people, to repair the injury of this deathlike coldness, & yet it never brought me into kind & equal relations, & persons never claimed from me little loving acts of sweetness, but only help in great immergencies [sic]. All this did not throw me into an agitated state of mind, nor cause me the least remorse (& this was only one more proof of my icy condition). I looked on it as a dreadful fact that the heart of a human being should be turned to stone. Then how unworthy was I of the privileges of the church. I determined to make a clean breast of it to my Blessed Director, take this heart out & let him see that it was all of stone; & calmly take the consequences. I supposed he would tell me that he should have known this before, that my Faith could not be worthy the name, & until warmth could melt my heart, I was unworthy of the communion of the Blessed Sacrament. The morng was beautiful, the birds singing, the sun rising as I walked through the still streets; & though I was traveling along with a load heavier than any poor beast of burden ever carried, yet I could not feel wretched though I thought I ought to be. I entered the Sacristy.... The boys said Bishop Hughes...was coming over soon. I trembled a little as I sat by the fire waiting for him. In a few minutes he came, bright & serene as the morng. I told him all; and more than I have told you, & what do you think he quietly said? "My child, this is not to cause you a moment's uneasiness, or a moment's thought; there is no sin in it, any more than that you are tall & not short. If you have ever consented to sin, when you had a moment to reflect on what you were doing, of this repent, for this, ask forgiveness; but that your heart is not tender, is no concern of yours. God does not ask from you what you have not. If you had been bred up in the church, perhaps habit & its various influences would have softened your nature." "Is there no hope now," said I? "That is not a question for you to ask nor for me to answer. Neither you nor I have anything to do with it. It is with God alone. Say to Him Oh God take this poor, cold heart of mine & make of it what thou wilt. You have nothing more to do." "But" I said "obedience is the first duty & I am told to love God & my neighbor." "Not with the heart you have not my child, but with the heart you have. Such states of mind are wholly independent of ourselves. And if you had all you ask, you would be a seraph, & you do not ask of God to be a seraph surely while you are on earth. This heart of yours is a cross which you must patiently bear to the end if needs be. You suffer in common with many of the Saints. Have you never read of St. Theresa, how she suffered for years with coldness & dryness of heart? A heart that melts away in affection even for God, is often an obstacle to steadfast fidelity in his service, & to the formation of the virtues of an heroic character. It is not that which will enable you to resist all the temptations of the world rather than utter a word of untruth. And if all the wealth of the world cannot tempt you from rectitude, let this satisfy you." At these words, which came to me as if from an angel, I passed, as it were from death unto Life. They were the words of God, & came to me as truth, absolute truth, & how comforting they were I need not tell you. When I asked my Rev. Father, if one who could read over the mysteries of the Passion of our Lord without emotion, was worthy of partaking of his Blessed Body. "What," said he, "could be more cold than the narration itself. The narrators did not feel it in its fullness. They relate it as they would something they met at a crossing of the road. Did you never notice this. Go to communion, my child in peace...as you & Julia so often say "How kind they are to us!" I knew it too, & yet a stroke of lightening could not have surprised me more than the first words with which my confession was met.[157]

This crisis may have been brought on in part by the accumulated fatigue resulting from Sophia's efforts at Brook Farm. It may have been a reaction from the exaltation experienced during her conversion. It may be that she had been overdoing the fasting in her first Lent as a Catholic. For she wrote:

> ...Do not you think the knowledge of self, comes as one of the graces of fasting? Certainly it is since the first week in Lent that this revelation has become more clear, & is becoming more clear every hour to me....[158]

She also told an amusing story at her own expense, of how she was delicately reprimanded by her Irish cook:

> Bridget & I went to Brooklyn to church this morng, & how delighted you would have been to hear her

reprove me for my puritannic condition. After introducing the subject by speaking of Lent, she says "I never saw anyone so changed as you have been since you have lived in Flatbush. You are thinner than any woman I ever saw, & so silent, & always by yourself, & when we lived at Brook Farm, I was as glad as I was to see the girls & boys when you came down to the house." "Why Bridget: [sic] said I, "I never was so happy in my life" "I know it" says she "because you have got something to be happy for, that you never had before, but I was telling Mrs. Dillon, over the way, the other day how you had changed, & she said people often did so when they first got into the church, & *you laid yourself down too hard to it at first*, & it was not good for you." "Well Biddy," said I, "I am very happy, but I am sorry you are not pleased & do not like me as well as you used to do." "Oh!" said she, "I like you a great deal better than usual, only you are so still!"[159]

There was a deeper cause, however, for Sophia's self reproach than any of the above. For years she had been unable to win her own father's love and approval. On August 5, 1849, she wrote:

…dear C- how is my poor, poor father? Sometimes it seems to me I must write a few lines of strong appeal to him not to leave me so, & perhaps relent when it is too late. If his heart were softened to me it might be softened to brighter influences. It will be a mournful recollection to me to take with me through my whole life, that of his unrelenting—cruel, & from anyone else I should say insulting neglect. & from the bottom of my heart I would say that I do not know anything I could have done through life towards him, different from what I have done.[160]

In March 1850 when she was planning a trip to Boston, she

added a little postscript to her letter:

> Will it not be possible for you to mention my intended
> visit to My Father—ask him in my name if he really
> wishes to end his days unreconciled to me—& if not
> what he requires me to do in order to regain his good
> will. As there is nothing I would not do for so desir-
> able an end but to commit a sin.[161]

For a person of Sophia Ripley's sensitivity this sense of
being unwanted by her father must have been a terrible psy-
chological experience. Because she was not "cold." How could
a person be cold who had written Charlotte, "You are so near
me always that I have to withdraw myself from you to
write"?[162] Or who had suffered such anguish at the death of
her brother? Even this very self-accusation of coldness was
proof, it would seem, of a passionately loving nature that
could never be satisfied with what it had to give. Bishop
Hughes must have felt this when he compared her to St.
Theresa and when he said, "If you had all you ask you would
be a seraph." Only, because her love was repulsed, Sophia
became shy and "reserved." And then in her generosity she
took the blame upon herself. Could anything be more pathetic
than that statement: "I saw that all my life I had been trying to
do good to people to repair the injury of this death like coldness and yet it never brought me into kind & equal relations"?

One phrase in this letter is very significant, it seems to me.
That is: "I saw that all through life my ties with others were
those of the intellect & imagination."[163] It does appear to have
been true that Sophia found difficulty in establishing and
maintaining really sympathetic relationships with people
with whom she could not be united intellectually. She continued to love them—but she loved them so much that the intellectual separation caused her intense pain. Sophia was not
tolerant by nature.

For this reason it was good for Sophia that her husband did
not share her religion with her. She grew tremendously in

understanding these last years of her life. She refrained from trying to convert him by argument, though "this is the hardest discipline of all I have ever suffered."[164] Instead she decided to offer her whole will to God and leave everything in his hands. In order that she might do this more perfectly she seems to have asked her confessor to become her director, and accepted a rule of life from him. In accordance with this rule her whole day, until her husband's return in the evening, was absorbed in good works.[165]

George Ripley's religious position in 1848 he explained in a letter to Orestes Brownson:

> …Let the authority be as absolute, as infallible as we
> can conceive it to be, our own perception of it is liable
> to error, — the moment Divine Truth comes in contact
> with a human mind, its nature may be changed….[166]

Therefore, by inference, he could not believe any church to be infallible. And he thought logical demonstration and argument on religion futile. People shoud set forth their religious views, but not try to prove them and answer objections. A man could only believe those truths which awoke an answering echo within himself.

No one could have been kinder or more considerate, however, than George Ripley was toward his wife. In 1849, when they were so poor, he gave her a gold piece to put in the "Peter's Pence" collection.[167] He bought her a picture of St. Elizabeth's miracle of the flowers.[168] He sold some of his books to buy her a set of the *Lives of the Saints.*[169] He went to church with her on occasion, and when she was ill arranged for a priest to bring her the Sacraments. Sometimes, when her friends were too insistent in their efforts to convert him, he would turn them aside with friendly jokes — as when he promised a Sister that he would go to church once if she would see to it that there was enough starch in his shirts for a whole month![170] Sophia repeated these jokes with relish in her letters to Charlotte. When George Ripley and Charles A.

Dana were editing their *New American Cyclopoedia*, they asked Catholics to write the articles on things Catholic. George Ripley and Archbishop Hughes became very good friends and the Archbishop headed the list of Catholic subscribers.[172] It is pleasant to think that the spirit of forbearance and charity which the Ripleys achieved in their marriage bore fruit in an increase of that spirit in American scholarship.

O. B. Frothingham says that Sophia Ripley, from the point of view of her new religion, came to think of the Brook Farm experiment as a mistake. There is little evidence on this point. She quite clearly thought she could not rightfully subscribe to Fourier's philosophy. From a Catholic point of view I suppose Fourier's doctrine would seem to teach: "Seek ye first all other things and the Kingdom of God and His justice shall be added unto you."[173] But that is not quite the same thing as thinking Brook Farm a mistake. On Saturday, April 1, 1848, she wrote:

> ...Great Fourier times now a days dear! Associationists taking a large share in regulating the late changes in France. Private letters coming from there all the time, cheering the brethren here with the assurance that an attempt will now be made for the reorganization of industry. All are in high spirits. Tonight a public demonstration of sympathy is to be made by them at the Minerva rooms Broadway. Mr. Ripley is all engaged in it, & will speak I suppose. The weather spares me the pain of going, which I should have done, for dear George's sake, if the Bishop thought it best. Perhaps something may be done by the French government, under the sanction of the church, to carry out parts of Fourier's mechanical arrangements for the benefit of the oppressed. But I never did sympathize in the least with the glorification of the man. Next week Friday comes off the birth-night party. It is to be given at rooms in Broadway, a supper and dance etc. with speeches. Tickets to be sold, which

gives it a very disagreeable publicity. The whole arrangement is not at all to my taste, & coming on a Friday in Lent I think I *must* be excused.[174] George will not urge it; but then he is so sad, at the thought of any separation of interest, that it is really a trial to me. Don't mention these things, dear, even to aunts, for there is not a human being to whom I can speak freely about them except to you. Perhaps I ought not even to you, as I cannot to George. It is a compensation to me when pained by separation from these friends of mine, and compelled to a withdrawal from them; to think that if any work can *rightfully* be done in their service, I am now going through a preparation which will help me to do it.[175]

There is, in fact, reason to believe that Sophia Ripley felt an affectionate remembrance for the spirit of Brook Farm and a kinship between what was there attempted and the spirit of a Catholic religious order. For when she went with Sarah Stearns to Mount St. Vincent, on the day that Sarah entered there as a Sister of Charity, she wrote:

> …We sat on the rocks under some trees & talked over old times before she took the irrevocable step of entering the house.…Something within & without seemed so like Brook Farm, that the whole was more a revival of some former experience than anything new & strange…[176]

Perhaps because of this feeling, Mrs. Ripley felt much drawn to the religious orders. In one letter she wrote: "Oh these blessed religious! I almost live at the Convent & have been happier all day because Mrs. Elwell dreamed last night that she saw me in the dress of a nun."[177] Another time she speaks of a certain nun looking "much as I myself should dressed in her garb."[178] Part of this attraction was undoubtedly that in the religious orders she found the parent-child relation which she had so much missed in her own life.[179] Since she could not be a nun herself, Sophia resolved to devote herself to working for those who were. And in this connection she wrote a short sentence that was really a description of the ideal to which she was faithful her whole life through: "why may my ambition not aspire to the highest title the Church has to give.—The servant of the servants of God?"[180]

In 1849 *The Harbinger* went bankrupt. In March George Ripley wrote John Sullivan Dwight:

> We are about leaving Flatbush, & indeed, already we are in New York most of the time at our old quarters in 9th St....Mrs. R. is at work in the establishment of her classes, with great encouragement from friends, & good prospects of success. I am still seeking a "sitervation" (how much it looks like starvation, that word) but as yet have had no decent offer, except a partial proposal from Greeley to work nearly the whole night at his office all the week long at $12. I may be induced to accept this, but I fear my health, at least for the present is hardly adequate.[181]

On April 6th he wrote again:

> For the last week, I have done little but vibrate on the road between here and Flatbush, winding up our affairs in that delectable Dutch residence...[182]

On April 29 Sophia wrote to Charlotte:

> Mr. Ripley was installed as assistant editor of the Tribune, which will give us a comfortable addition to our means of living; engage him in a department of literary criticism that he enjoys very much, & leave him plenty of time for other occupations; besides giving him at once a fixed position which you know is very desirable.[183]

The Ripley idea of a "comfortable" income can be inferred

from the fact that at this period he was paid $5 every other week by the *Tribune*! They lived in a boarding house at a Mrs. Elwell's, 4 Amity Street. Sophia' plan to start another school did not work out. On October 29th she wrote:

> I have no pupils as yet. I have done all I can in a private way — & shall not at present make any more effort. So many persons know of my plan that I think something will come of it in the course of the season.
>
> Meanwhile the rest is perfectly delicious. The first I ever had in my life.

Sophia's idea of a rest was remarkably strenuous. Despite a headache she had spent most of the preceding week at the hospital of the Sisters of Charity making bed linen. And she had just finished her two-volume translation of *Religion in Society*. She wrote in August that it was "coming on" and that the Bishop was reading it preparatory to writing the preface.

Besides this first book, Sophia seems to have translated St. Alphonsus Liguon's *Glories of Mary*, which Father Hecker recommended to her.[184] She also wrote occasional reviews of lectures for the Tribune[185] and translated articles from the French paper *l'Ami de la Religion* for the *Freeman's Journal*.[186] She wrote also of other translations of selected spiritual writers, as well as English titles for some holy pictures. Finally she translated the *Life and Doctrines of St. Catherine of Genoa*.[187] St. Catherine was a sixteenth-century married woman who worked as a volunteer in the hospital at Genoa. Her most interesting teachings were about Purgatory. She taught that it was the love of God working in the soul which made both the pain and the joy of Purgatory: joy because the soul is so attracted by God's goodness, pain because its imperfections keep it from union with its Beloved. And some souls, she taught, feel this purifying joy and pain even on earth. This last book was not published until thirteen years after Sophia Ripley's death. Father Hecker wrote in the Introduction:

It was fitting that the life of Saint Catherine of Genoa should be translated for the first time into English, by one who is now no more, but who was while living, distinguished, like our saint, for her intellectual gifts, for her charity toward the poor and abandoned, and in consecrating her pen to the cause and glory of God's Church.[188]

Besides her work in the hospitals, Sophia Ripley visited the city's prisons, insane asylums and reformatories.[189] She was particularly interested in the rehabilitation of young girls who had gotten into trouble. Realizing how difficult things were for these girls, who often were foreign born, poor and friendless, and who had to overcome the stigma of having been in prison, Sophia and some friends who worked with her persuaded Archbishop Hughes to bring the Sisters of the Good Shepherd to New York. These nuns treat such girls with friendliness and understanding and teach them to be self-supporting. The story is that Archbishop Hughes was skeptical of the possibility of effecting permanent reform of women who had "gone wrong." Moreover he was already harassed with money worries and did not want to bring a new religious order to New York. Miss Foster, the matron of The Tombs, and a non-Catholic, won him over. "'But, Archbishop,' said Miss Foster, 'would you consider the work a failure if but one grievous sin were prevented?…Would not this be to the honor of God?'" The Archbishop capitulated![190]

Sophia Ripley chose the home for the new order, brought them their first "penitent" and begged for their support, for eight hours a day in all kinds of weather, until they were well established.[191] Between 1857 and 1861 she collected over $3,000.[192]

In 1855 Sophia's father died. As he got older he had become more and more irresponsible. Eventually he seems to have become definitely insane. The last year of his life the family thought of putting him in an asylum.[193] He remained obdurate in his refusal to see Sophia, despite appeals and letters from her. Her sister, Mary Elizabeth, too, would neither speak to Sophia nor let her see her father. She tried to comfort herself by throwing herself into her social work:

> …It has sometimes seemed strange that I am called to minister in my small way to the wants & comforts of strangers, & am not allowed to approach those who have a natural claim upon me; but I begin to see it in a different light now, & how it is all the same in the true Catholic sense; that we must minister to those whom we see suffering by our side & someone else will do for those we especially love from whom we are divided…[194]

Sophia felt it to be a religious duty to be composed and detached—but she loved her relatives so intensely that she found this very difficult to do. After her father's death the tension eased up. Sophia and Mary Elizabeth became friends again also.

In 1859 Mrs. Ripley injured her breast, while stooping to pick up something behind her marble topped bureau.[195] A cancer developed. She was operated upon in June 1860. She accepted her illness in the same matter-of-fact spirit in which she had accepted the Brook Farm experiment. On July 5th she wrote to Charlotte Dana that she was very much embarrassed because her friends insisted on treating her "like a princess," and because they commiserated with her: "Where is their faith?" In August her husband took her to Staten Island to recuperate in the sea breezes. Mary Elizabeth stayed with them. They enjoyed trips on the ferry, and listening to the salute of the ships as they came in. They nursed George through an attack of rheumatism. Sophia's strength seemed to return.[196] In the fall they took a trip to New England to visit the Danas at Manchester-by-the-Sea. Sophia's last letter was written on the eve of this visit:

Will not Richard join us, as he more than half promised to do? I know you will be glad to have him, & then what a thankful happy little company we shall be, with Aunty & your father at the head.…With love to all, from us both till we meet & always.[197]

On their return the disease broke out again in full strength. Sophia bore her suffering gently.[198] Her husband had a photograph made of her in her sick-bed, and a portrait painted from it by Richard Morrell Staigg.[199] Probably they had never had enough money for such a thing before. On February 4, 1861 she died. George took her body to Boston. The funeral was in his old Purchase Street Church, which had in the meantime been turned into a Catholic Church.[200] Sophia was buried in the Dana family tomb, in the Old Burying Ground, near Harvard Square.

On his return to New York George Ripley wrote to "Aunt Betsy":

> New York seems to me like a solitary city, and its streets are almost thronged with spectres, now that I no longer see the dear and pleasant face which alone gave interest to life in these busy crowds.[201]

And to Richard Henry Dana, Sr., he wrote of Sophia:

> Her disposition was absolutely faultless; sometimes quick in her temper and her words, as she always was in her perceptions, she had not a trace of ill-will to a human being in her nature. Impatient by physical temperament, she was singularly gentle and forbearing in action; always a peace maker by instinct; and with a native delicacy that enabled her to meet almost every variety of character with justice and love. Her religious faith was meek and confiding as that of a child towards the most tender parent and in no emergency did it falter for a moment. Surely such perfect unworldliness, such wonderful freedom from selfish-

ness, such singular integrity both of mind and heart, such a lofty spirit combined with such sweet womanly grace, were never found in so beautiful a union before.[202]

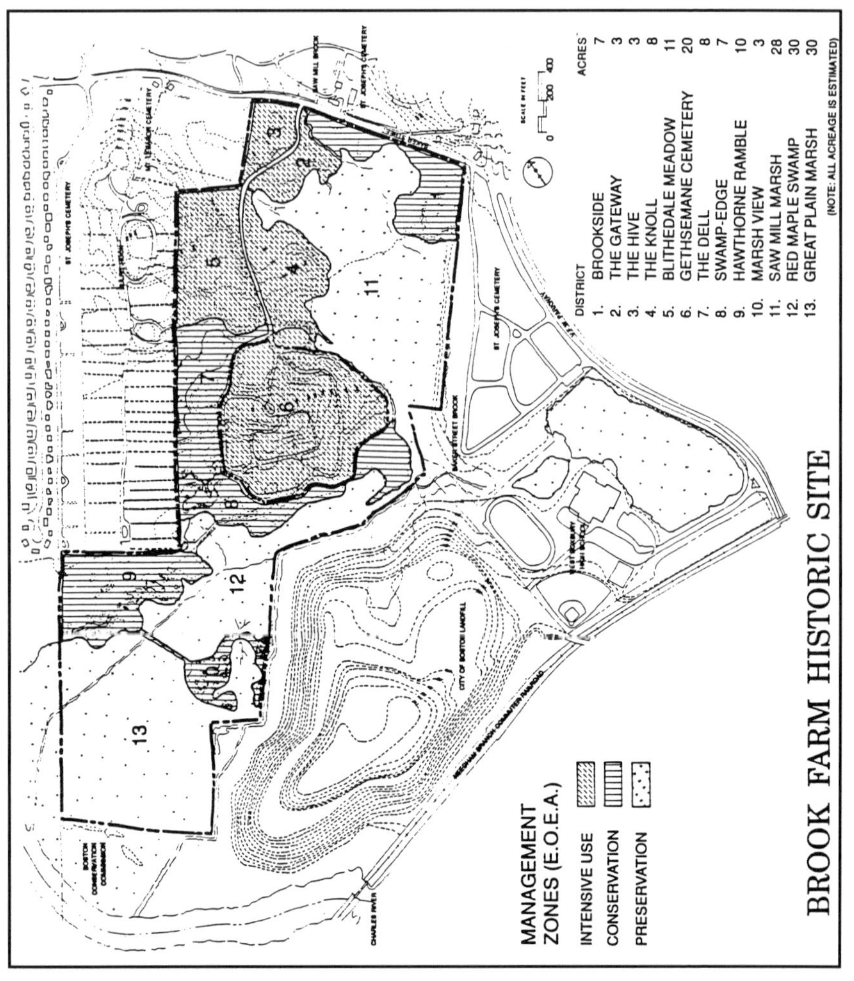

Brook Farm Historic Site, Management Zones, 1990 Collection of the West Roxbury Historical Society

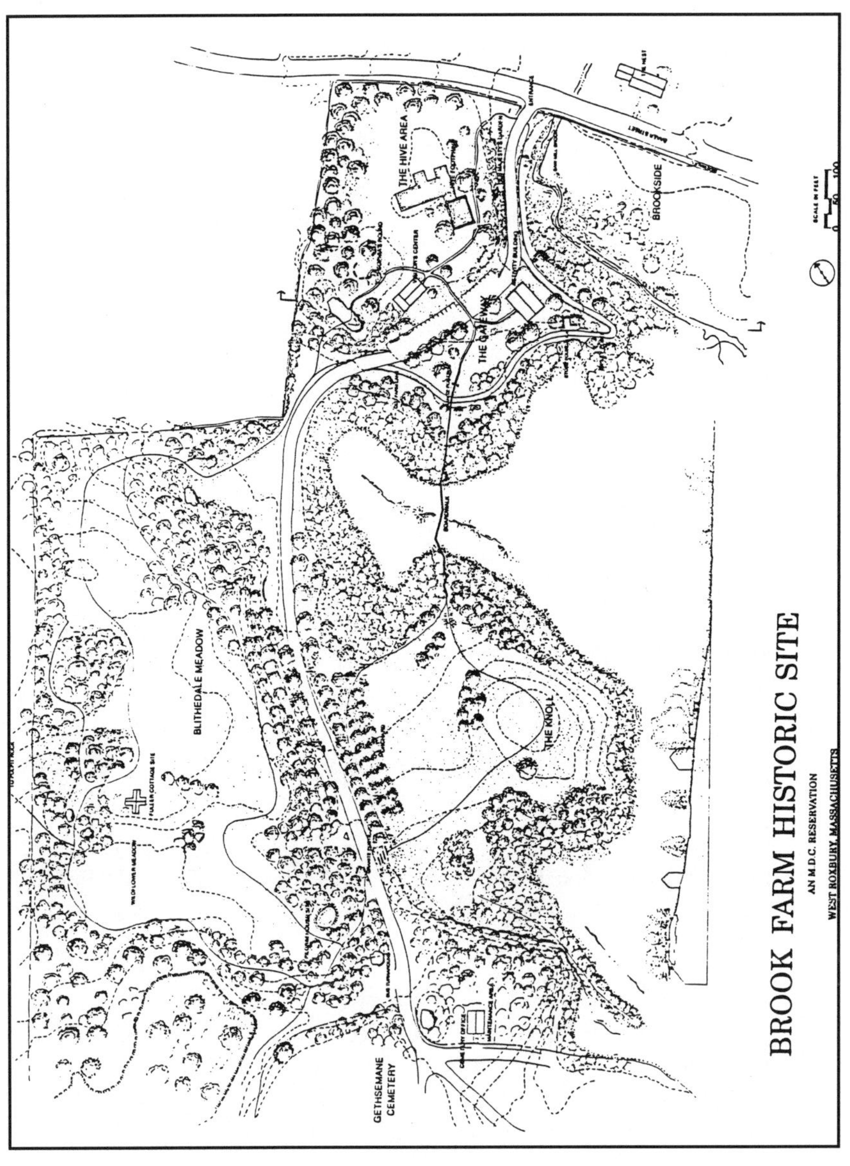

Brook Farm Historic Site, Historic Site Zone, 1990 Collection of the West Roxbury Historical Society

Appendix

Father Hecker's
"Tribute to Mrs. George Ripley."[203]

Time, which reconciles us to so many losses, makes other but more deeply felt. Deep was the grief with which the announcement of Mrs. Geo. Ripley's death first fell upon her friends and acquaintances, but after the lapse of more than a year since that event, there are those among us who still find new reasons to remember her with regret. Such persons will understand why I attempt to pay another tribute to her worth and excellence.

I met Mrs. Ripley first at Brook Farm in the year 1843. During the nine months of my stay there, though I had not an opportunity to form a very intimate acquaintance with her, I saw enough to recognize in her a highly intellectual woman who concealed under a habitual reserve the most elevated sentiments and deepest affections. Her desire to realize a social life more noble and Christian than was ordinarily practiced in the world, led her to take a full share in the menial duties of the establishment, but her striking dignity of manner, partly the effect of native grace, and partly of her strong high purposes, accompanied her through all.

Two years afterwards[204] on my way to New York I spent an evening with Mr. & Mrs. Ripley at Brook Farm. It was just after I had come to the determination to enter the Catholic Church, and the conversation turned mostly on my reasons for that step. Both listened with interest, but Mrs. Ripley betrayed a warmth and earnestness of feeling, the more remarkable for its contrast to her ordinaliry (sic) unexcited manner, which impressed me with the belief that a change had taken place in her life, and the hope that she might one day become a Catholic.

My impressions turned out to be not unfounded, for in 1847 while pursuing my studies for the priesthood in Europe, I received a letter from Mrs. Ripley, announcing her conversion to the Catholic Church. The hope, the gushing joy with which this letter was full would be hard to describe. Her strong nature which had been hitherto confined and restrained was suddenly unlocked. The veil which had enveloped her was torn away, and her character stood out in all its life and warmth. On my return to the United States, I had the privilege, as I deem it, of being chosen as her confessor,[205] and from that time almost up to the hour of her death was fully acquainted with the development of her religious character.

Her attachment to the Catholic Church was very deep. She did not enter it from any passing excitement. Her imagination, taste and feelings were all too much under the control of her reason for her to allow their undue weight in deciding her to take such a step. It was her deep felt want of the assistance of God's Grace, and her profound conviction that the Church was the dispenser of that grace that, in spite of every worldly consideration, led her to enter its fold. From that moment her faith in the Church was complete and unwavering. Its doctrines and mysteries were the food of her intelligence. Its altars the tabernacles of her Saviour, at which it was her happiness to kneel every day, and often in the week to nourish her soul with the Bread of Life. Its Saints were her friends and companions. To Saint Francis of Assisi, the sweet model of humility, simplicity and charity, she had a particular devotion, speaking of him as if she had seen and known him, and enrolling herself not long before her death, in fulfillment of a long cherished desire, as his child and disciple in the society known as the 'Third Order of St. Francis.' That fastidiousness which is so often the accompaniment of high culture, never appeared in her as a Catholic, but in its place there was an unconscious humility that led her to adopt the most simple and ordinary devotions of the Church. Her fondness for the pictures of our Lord and the Saints and for the grandeur of the Church services was almost that of a child. She was accustomed to recite the Rosary of the B. Virgin every day, and the 'Stations of the Cross' drew her to the church every Friday, to kneel on the pavement with the common people, following our Saviour step by step on his painful path to Calvary. With all this, as might be expected, she united the most fervent desire for the spread of the Catholic faith. There was hardly a conversation in which this desire did not express itself, and it was this that led her to translate into English, several works calculated to diffuse a true knowledge of Catholic doctrines and practices. The last thing she did, when I saw her just before her death, was to whisper in my ear, with a beaming face, her hopes of the conversion of a very near and dear relative.

But the most distinguishing feature of her Catholic life was her charity. This seemed to be unbounded. Certainly, it was not limited by her bodily strength. The poor, the sick, the little children in our City Institutes, particularly those on Randall's Island, were the object of her laborious and systematic care, up to her last illness. Not content with consoling and instructing them while they were inmates of these establishments, she continued in numberless cases, to aid them after they left, doing all in her power to rescue them from wretchedness. She had a wonderful zeal for reclaiming abandoned women, and it was owing chiefly to her exertions that the Sisters of the Good Shepherd were brought for that purpose. For years and years she begged for their support, and often even in the heats of mid-summer, regardless of comfort and almost of health, she spent the day going from store to store in the lower part of the city, to solicit aid for this noble charity. Nor did all these continued labors exhaust her zeal. When any new cases of suffering came up, some poor child to be looked after, some erring woman to be snatched from ruin, she gave herself to the task with an energy as fresh as if she had nothing to do, and a perseverance which was satisfied with nothing but success. In fact, so abundant was her life in good works, so high in purpose, and so self-sacrificing that it was with perfect truth and sincerity I said to her on her deathbed: 'My dear Friend, if God should restore you again to health, I would not know how to give you any better advice than simply to recommend you to take up again your labors of love at the point where your illness compelled you to break them off.'

I regard Mrs. Ripley's conversion as a striking testimony to the power of Catholic truth over a clear mind, a strong will, early prejudices, and the opposition of the world. I believe that the grace to believe was accorded to her by Heaven in reward for the straightforwardness, earnestness and purity with which she labored at Brook Farm to carry out the precepts of this charity. And I regard her Catholic life as a beautiful exemplification of the Spirit and teaching of the Church. She is that "valiant woman," of whom the Holy Scripture speaks. "Her works praise her in the gates, and her children"—the orphan whose tears she dried, and the outcast and abandoned to whom she brought back hope and virtue—"rise up and call her blessed."

Bibliography

MANUSCRIPT SOURCES

Brook Farm. Records in Massachusetts Historical Society, Boston, Massachusetts.

Bancroft Papers. Massachusetts Historical Society, Boston, Massachusetts. Contains many letters from George Ripley.

Brownson Papers. University of Notre Dame, South Bend, Indiana. Mostly letters sent to Brownson. Some rough drafts of letters he wrote. His early diary. One letter from Sophia Ripley. Contains also letters from George Ripley and many letters mentioning the Ripleys.

Channing Papers. Boston Public Library, Boston Massachusetts. Contains material about Brook Farm, and an important letter about George and Sophia Ripley from Margaret Fuller.

Dana Papers. Massachusetts Historical Society, Boston, Massachusetts. Contains a long series of letters from Sophia Ripley to Ruth Charlotte Dana, 1846–1860. Also letters from George Ripley to various Danas.

Dana, Elizabeth Ellery. Letters to Vivien May Norris, 1900. Radcliffe College, Cambridge, Massachusetts.

Dana, Isabella. Copies of parts of a letter to Elizabeth Ellery Dana, October, 1928. Radcliffe College, Cambridge, Massachusetts. Contains description of Sophia Ripley.

Dana, Ruth Charlotte. Memorandum dictated to her niece, Mrs. Rosemond Dana Wild, 1890. Property of Henry Wadsworth Longfellow Dana, Longfellow House, Cambridge, Massachusetts.

Dwight Papers. Boston Public Library, Boston, Massachusetts. Letters to John Sullivan Dwight. A gold mine of information on Transcendentalists and on Brook Farm. Contains four important letters from Sophia Ripley.

Emerson, Ralph Waldo. Emerson Memorial Association Papers. Houghton Library, Harvard University, Cambridge, Massachusetts. Contains two important letters form Sophia Ripley, 1843.

Frothingham Collection. Massachusetts Historical Society, Boston, Massachusetts. Some of the papers used by O. B. Frothingham in preparing his book on George Ripley.

Fuller Papers. Houghton Library, Harvard University, Cambridge, Massachusetts. Contains four letters from Sophia Ripley. Also letters mentioning the Ripleys.

Hecker Papers. Paulist Fathers' Archives, New York City. Contains diaries, memoranda and notes, as well as letters from and to Isaac Hecker. Contain manuscript, "A Tribute to Mrs. George Ripley." There are also references to her in the diary and letters.

Longfellow Papers. Longfellow House, Cambridge, Massachusetts. Contains four letters from Sophia Ripley to Henry Wadsworth Longfellow.

Lowell, James Russell. Manuscript autobiography written for his class records in 1838. Harvard College, Cambridge, Massachusetts.

Massachusetts General Court. House Journal, May, 1829 — March, 1830, vol. 50. Massachusetts State Library, Boston, Massachusetts.

Middlesex County Courthouse, Cambridge, Massachusetts. Records, 1811.

Ripley, George. "A Common Place Book, upon the Plan Recommended by John Locke, Esq." Houghton Library, Harvard University, Cambridge, Massachusetts.

_____ Six scrapbooks containing his newspaper and magazine articles. Houghton Library, Harvard University, Cambridge, Massachusetts.

Ripley, Sophia Willard Dana. Letters to Lydia Hobart Ripley. In possession of Mrs. Jeter Isely, Princeton, New Jersey.

_____ Letter addressed "Dear Sir," October 29 (1857). In possession of Frederic Woolsey Pratt, Concord, Massachusetts.

Sherman, Rose. Notes of an interview with Elizabeth Ellery Dana, 1928. Radcliffe College, Cambridge, Massachusetts.

PRINTED SOURCES

Alcott, Amos Bronson. *Journals* (ed. Odell Shepard). Boston: Little, Brown and Company, 1938.

Bradford, George Partridge. "Reminiscences of Brook Farm by a

Member of the Community," *Century Magazine*, XLV, no. 1 (November, 1892), pp. 141–148.

Brisbane, Albert. *Social Destiny of Man*. Philadelphia: C.F. Stollmeyer, 1840.

Brook Farm Association. *Constitution of the Brook Farm Association for Industry and Education*. Boston: 1844.

Brook Farm Phalanx. *Constitution of the Brook Farm Phalanx, Adopted May 1, 1845*. West Roxbury, 1845.

Brownson, Orestes A. *The Convert, or Leaves from My Experience*. New York: Edward Dunigan and Brother, 1857.

Brownson, Orestes A. *The Works of Orestes A. Brownson* (ed. Henry F. Brownson). Detroit: Thorndike House, 1884.

Catalogue Forum Qui in Universitate Harvardiana Cantabrigiae in Republica Massachusettensi ab Anno MDCXLII ad Annum MDCCCIII Alicujus Gradus Laurea donati sunt. Cantabrigiae e Universitatis Typographeo Gulielmo Hilliard, 1803.

Codman, John T. *Brook Farm: Historic and Personal Memoirs*, Boston: Arena Publishing Company, 1894.

Curtis, George W. *Early Letters of George W. Curtis to John S. Dwight, Brook Farm and Concord*, (ed. George Willie Cooke). New York and London: Harper and Bros., 1898.

Dall, Caroline H. *Margaret and her Friends or Ten Conversations with Margaret Fuller upon the Mythology of the Greeks and its Expression in Art*. Boston: Roberts Brothers, 1895.

The Dial: a Magazine for Literature, Philosophy, and Religion. (ed. Sarah Margaret (Fuller) Ossoli, Ralph Waldo Emerson, George Ripley), Vol. I–IV (July, 1840–April, 1844). Boston: Weeks, Jordan, and Company: London: Wiley and Putnam, 1841–1844.

Dwight, Marianne. *Letters from Brook Farm, 1844–1847* (ed. Amy L. Reed). Poughkeepsie, New York: Vassar College, 1928.

Emerson, Ralph Waldo. *Journals of Ralph Waldo Emerson* (ed. Edward W. Emerson and Waldo Emerson Forbes). Boston: Houghton, Mifflin Company, 1909–1912.

The Letters of Ralph Waldo Emerson (ed. Ralph L. Rusk). New York: Columbia University Press, 1939.

The Works of Ralph Waldo Emerson. "Standard Library Edition." Boston and New York: Houghton, Mifflin and Company, 1883.

Fourier, Francois Charles Marie. *The Social Destiny of Man; or Theory of the Four Movements* (translated by Henry Clapp Jr.) with a

Treatise on the Function of the Human Passions and an Outline of Fourier's System of Social Science by Albert Brisbane. New York: Robert M. Dewitt, 1857.

Greeley, Horace. *Recollections of a Busy Life*. New York: J.B. Ford, 1868.

The Harbinger, Devoted to Social and Political Progress. Vols. I—IV published by Brook Farm Phalanx. New York: Burgess, Stringer, and Company. Boston: Redding and Company, 1843–1847. After vol. IV transferred to the American Union of Associationists, and published in New York until February, 1849.

Hawthorne, Nathaniel. *Passages from the American Notebooks*. Boston and New York: Houghton, Mifflin and Company, 1886.

The American Notebooks by Nathaniel Hawthorne, based upon the Original Manuscripts in the Pierpont Morgan Library (ed. Randall Stewart). New Haven: Yale University Press; London: M. Milford, Oxford University Press, 1932.

Hecker, Isaac T. *Aspirations of Nature*. New York: James B. Kirker, 1857.

The Church and the Age. New York: Office of the Catholic World, 1887.

Questions of the Soul. New York: D. Appleton and Company, 1854.

"The Transcendental Movement in New England," *Catholic Review*, XXIII (1876), pp. 528–537.

Kirby, Georgianna Bruce. *Years of Experience*. New York and London: G.P. Putnam's Sons, 1887.

Liguori, St. Alphonsus. *The Glories of Mary*, translated from the Italian (probably by Sophia Willard Dana Ripley). New York: Edward Dunigan and Brother, 1852.

Life and Doctrine of Saint Catharine of Genoa, translated from the Italian (by Sophia Willard Dana Ripley). New York: The Catholic Publication Society, 1874.

Martinet, Abbe Antoine. *Religion in Society, or the Solution of Great Problems: Placed within the Reach of Every Mind*, translated from the French (by Sophia Willard Dana Ripley). New York: D. and J. Sadlier, 1850.

Massachusetts General Court. "An Act to Incorporate Brook Farm," *Acts and Resolve Passed by the General Court of Massachusetts 1845*, chapter 169.

New York Freeman's Journal and Catholic Register. New York: 1840–1911.

Broken files in St. Joseph's Seminary, Dunwoodie, New York, and in the American Antiquarian Society, Worcester, Massachusetts. Complete file in Dominican house of Studies, Catholic University of America, Washington, D.C.

Norton, Andrews. *The Latest Form of Infidelity*. Cambridge: J. Owen, 1837.

Peabody, Elizabeth. "A Glimpse of Christ's Idea of Society," *The Dial*, II, no. 2 (October, 1841), pp. 214–223.

Last Evening with Allston, and other Papers, Boston: D. Lothrop and Company, 1886.

"Plan of the West Roxbury Community," *The Dial*, II, no. 3 (January, 1842), pp. 361–372.

The Phalanx, A Journal of Social Science. New York: J. Winchester, 1843–1844. Continued as *The Harbinger*.

Ripley, George. *Claims of the Age on the work of the Evangelist; a Sermon Preached at the Ordination of Mr. John Sullivan Dwight, as Pastor of the Second Congregational Church in Northampton, May 20, 1840*. Boston: Weeks, Jordan, and Company, 1840.

A Letter to Mr. Andrews Norton, Occasioned by his Discourse before the Association of the Alumni of the Cambridge Theological School, on the 19th of July, 1839. Boston: James Munroe and Company, 1839.

Letters on the Latest Forms of Infidelity, Including a View of the Opinions of Spinoza, Schleiermacher, and De Wette. Boston: James Munroe and Company, 1840.

Ripley, George (with Charles A. Dana) *The New American Cyclopaedia*. New York: D. Appleton and Company, 1858–1863, 16 vols.

Specimens of Foreign Standard Literature. vols. 1–11, Boston: Hilliard, Gray and Company, 1838–1841; vols. 12–14, Boston: James Munroe and Company, 1842.

Ripley, Sophia Willard Dana. "Letter," *The Dial*, II, no. 1 (July, 1841), pp. 122–129.

"Painting and Sculpture," *The Dial*, II, no. 1 (July, 1841), pp. 78–81.

"Woman," *The Dial*, I, no. 3 (January, 1841), pp. 362–366.

Russell, Amelia, "Home Life of the Brook Farm Association," *Atlantic Monthly*, XLII (1878), pp. 458–466; 556-563.

Home Life of the Brook Farm Association. Boston: Little, Brown and Company, 1900. A reprint in book form of the Atlantic Monthly articles.

Sears, John Van Der Zee. *My Friends at Brook Farm*. New York: Desmond FitzGerald, Inc., 1912.

Sedgwick, Ora Gannett. "A Girl of Sixteen at Brook Farm," *Atlantic Monthly*, LXXXV (March, 1900), pp. 394-404.

"Girl's Recollections of the Brook Farm School," *Overland Monthly*, N.S. LXXII (September, 1918), p. 233.

Sumner, Arthur. "A Boy's Recollections of Brook Farm," *New England Magazine, NS. X, (May, 1894), pp. 309-313.*

SECONDARY WORKS

Allen, Joseph Henry. *Our Liberal Movement in Theology, chiefly as Shown in Recollections of the History of Unitarianism in New England,* Boston: Roberts Brothers, 1883.

Arnold, Harold Greene. *The Unitarian Spring at Brook Farm*, "Proceedings of the Unitarian Historical Society." Boston: Unitarian Historical Society, 1942.

Baker, Christina Hopkinson. *The Story of Fay House*. Cambridge: Harvard University Press, 1929.

Bestor, Arthur Eugene. "Albert Brisbane, Propagandist for Socialism in the 1840's," *New York History*, XXVIII (April, 1947), pp. 128-158.

"The Evolution of the Socialist Vocabulary," *Journal of the History of Ideas*, IX, no. 3 (June, 1948), pp. 259-302.

"Publication of Original Records of Brook Farm," *New England Quarterly* (March, 1940). Professor Bestor is collecting and editing records and letters from Brook Farm with a view to publication.

Brisbane, Redelia. Albert Brisbane, *A Mental Biography, by his Wife*. Boston: Arena Publishing Company, 1893.

Brooks, Van Wyck. *The Flowering of New England*. New York: E.P. Dutton, 1936.

Burton, Katherine. *Paradise Planters*. New York: Longmans, Green and Company, 1939. Fictionalized history of Brook Farm.

Burton, Katherine. "Sophia Dana Ripley," *Missionary*, LXIII (February, 1939), p. 40. Based on available printed sources.

Brownson, Henry F. *Orestes A. Brownson's Early Life*. Detroit: Nourse, 1898.

Clarke, J. F., Emerson, R. W., Channing, W. H. *Margaret Fuller, Marchesa d'Ossoli, Memoirs*. Boston: Phillips, Sampson and Company, 1852, 22 vols.

Coleman, Caryl, "Forgotten Convert: Sophia Ripley, Co-founder of Brook Farm," *Catholic World*, CXXII (November, 1925), p. 192. Based on available printed sources and on the Hecker Papers. Some inaccuracies.

Commager, Henry Steele. *Theodere Parker*. Boston: Little, Brown and Company, 1936.

Conway, Katherine. *In the Footprints of the Good Shepherd*. New York: 1857-1907.

Cooke, George Willis, "Brook Farm," *New England Magazine*, N.S. XVII (1897) , p. 391.

"The Dial": an Historical and Biographical Introduction, with a List of the Contributors, *The Journal of Speculative Philosophy*, XIX, No. 3(July, 1885) pp. 225-265.

John Sullivan Dwight, Brook Farmer, Editor, and Critic of Music. Boston: Small, Maynard and Company, 1898.

Unitarianism in America, a History of its Origin and Development. Boston: American Unitarian Association, 1902.

Curti, Merle Eugene. *The Growth of American Thought*. New York: Harper and Brothers, 1943.

Curtis, Georgina Pell. *Some Roads to Rome in America*. St. Louis: B. Herder, 1909.

Dana, Henry Wadsworth Longfellow. *The Dana Saga, Three Centuries of the Dana Family in Cambridge*. The Cambridge Historical Society, 1941, Cambridge: Harvard University Press, 1941.

Driscoll, Annette S. "A Brook Farm Convert Sophia Ripley," *Ave Maria*, XXXI (New Series), June 7, 1930, Notre Dame, Indiana.

Elliott, Walter. *The Life of Father Hecker*. New York: The Columbus Press, 1894.

Frothingham, Octavius B. *George Ripley*. Boston: Houghton, Mifflin and Company, 1882.

Transcendentalism in New England. New York: G. P. Putnam's Sons, 1876.

Goddard, H. C. *Studies in New England Transcendentalism*. "Columbia University Studies in English," Series II, no. 3. New York: Columbia University Press, 1907.

Haraszti, Zoltman. *The Idyll of Brook Farm, as Revealed by Unpublished Letters in the Boston Public Library*. Boston: Trustees of the Boston Public Library, 1940.

Hawthorne, Nathaniel. *The Blithedale Romance*. Boston: Tickner and Fields, 1868, 2 vols. Novel based on experiences at Brook Farm. Not to be used for accuracy!

Holden, Rev. Vincent F.C.S.P. *The Early Years of Isaac Thomas Hecker (1819-1844)*. Washington: Catholic University of America Press, 1939. A careful study.

Maynard, Theodore. *Orestes Brownson, Yankee, Radical, Catholic*. New York: MacMillan Company, 1943. Sound and also readable. Gives more attention to Brownson's life and thought after his conversion to Catholicism than does Schlesinger's book.

Metzdorf, Robert F. "Hawthorne's Suit against Ripley and Dana," Reprint from *American Literature* XII, no. 2 (May, 1940)

Morison, S. E. *Three Centuries of Harvard 1636-1936*. "Harvard University Series." Cambridge, 1936.

Paige, Lucius R. *History of Cambridge Massachusetts 1630-1877*. Boston: H. O. Houghton and Company: New York: Hurd and Houghton, 1877.

Palmer, Joseph (ed.) *Necrology of Alumni of Harvard College 1851-52 to 1862-63*. Boston: John Wilson and Son, 1864.

Parrington, Vernon Louis. *American Dreams: a Study of American Utopias*. "Brown University Studies" vol. II. Providence: Brown University, 1947.

Parrington, Vernon Louis. *Main Currents in American Thought*. 3 vols. in 1. New York: Harcourt Brace and Company, 1927-1930.

Riggs, Lisette. "George and Sophia Ripley." Unpublished Ph.D. dissertation, University of Maryland, 1942. The most thorough study yet made of George Ripley. The author, now Mrs. Jeter Isely, is preparing a book on George Ripley now, which will be very valuable. The dissertation is also the most careful study yet made of Sophia Ripley. Some new source material has come to light since it was written.

Schlesinger, Arthur M., Jr. *Orestes A. Brownson; a Pilgrim's Progress*. Boston: Little, Brown and Company, 1939. Scholarly and fascinatingly written. Not much attention devoted to Brownson's later life.

Schneider, Herbert Wallace. *A History of American Philosophy*. New York: Columbia University Press, 1946.

Swift, Lindsay. *Brook Farm, its Members, Scholars and Visitors*. New York, London: MacMillan Company, 1900. Still the best general account of Brook Farm.

Tyler, Alice Felt. *Freedom's Ferment: Phases of American Social History to 1860*. Minneapolis: University of Minnesota Press, 1944.

Weiss, John. *Life and Correspondence of Theodore Parker*. 2 vols. New York: Appleton, 1864.

Wilbur, Earl More. *Our Unitarian Heritage, an Introduction to the History of the Unitarian Movement*. Boston: Beacon Press, 1925.

Wilson, Howard Aaron. "George Ripley: Social and Literary Critic." Unpublished Ph.D. dissertation, University of Wisconsin, 1941.

Winsor, Justin (ed.) *The Memorial History of Boston*, vol. IV, Boston: Ticknor and Company, 1886.

Notes

1. H. W. L. Dana, *The Dana Saga* ("The Cambridge Historical Society"; Cambridge: Harvard University Press, 1941), pp. 20–31.

2. S. E. Morison, *Three Centuries of Harvard 1636–1936* ("Harvard University Series"; Cambridge: Harvard University Press, 1936), p. 174. The original pen-and-ink sketches now in possession of H. W. L. Dana, at the Longfellow House, Cambridge, Massachusetts.

3. Quoted from "Notes of an interview with Miss Elizabeth Dana, 15 Appian Way made by Miss Rose Sherman in 1928" (now in possession of Radcliffe College). The above Elizabeth Dana, who has since died, was the daughter of R. H. Dana, Jr., and was the family genealogist.

4. Date of birth inscribed on the tomb of the Dana family, Cambridge Burying Ground, Garden Street, Cambridge.

5. Dana, *The Dana Saga*, p. 29 says that these speculations consisted in the building of docks and wharves in Cambridgeport, which Francis thought would become the most important seaport in America. One wonders what the family opinion of Francis might have been, had his guess proved correct!

6. *Necrology of Alumni of Harvard College 1851–52 to 1862–63*, ed. Joseph Palmer, (Boston: John Wilson and Son, 1864), pp. 26–27. Consult also "Notes of an interview with Miss Elizabeth Dana, 15 Appian Way made by Miss Rose Sherman in 1928."

7. Middlesex County Courthouse, Cambridge, Massachusetts, Records, Entry of Cambridge 17th May 1811:

> To the Hon. James Prescott Esq. Judge of Probate for the County of Middlesex.
>
> This certifies, that, whereas my husband, Francis Dana, is absent in a foreign country, it becomes expedient for me to request that a guardian may be appointed for my children, as heirs to a portion of the Estate of the late Francis Dana Esq.—these children being minors under fourteen years of age. I do accordingly request your Honour, that my brother, Sidney Willard, may be appointed guardian to my children.
>
> Sophia Dana
granted

8. "Memorandum dictated by Ruth Charlotte Dana to her niece,

Rosamond Dana Wild, in 1890" (now in possession of H.W.L. Dana at the Longfellow House, Cambridge).

9. Probably Dr. James Jackson, author of "Letters to a Young Physician." He was a classmate of Francis Dana Jr. at Harvard (1796).

10. Sophia Willard Dana Ripley, letter to Ruth Charlotte Dana, Flatbus, Long Island, "Feria Tertia post Dominican infra Octavam Ascensionis" [June 7, 1848] (now in Massachusetts Historical Society, Dana Collection). Hereafter all letters of Sophia, unless otherwise designated, belong to the Dana Collection.

11. Elizabeth Dana, letter to Vivien May Norris, February 15, 1900. The letter states that she has received the information in a letter from Ruth Charlotte Dana.

12. "Memorandum dictated by Ruth Charlotte Dana to her niece, Rosamond Dana Wild, in 1890" (now in the possession of H. W. L. Dana at the Longfellow House, Cambridge).

13. *Ibid*.

14. Elizabeth Ellery Dana, letter to Vivien May Norris, February 15, 1900 (now in possession of Radcliffe College).

15. Mauscript autobiography of James Russell Lowell, written for his class records (now in possession of Harvard College).

16. Elizabeth Ellery Dana, letter to Vivien May Norris, February 17, 1900, quotes the above as being in a letter just received from her aunt, Ruth Charlotte Dana.

17. Ednah D. Cheney, "The Women of Boston," *Memorial History of Boston*, ed. Justin Winsor (Boston: Ticknor and Co., 1886), IV. 346.

18. "Notes of an interview with Miss Elizabeth Dana, 15 Appian Way made by Miss Rose Sherman, in 1928." In 1900 Miss Dana was less certain. At that time she wrote: "I have another letter from my aunt Ruth Charlotte Dana in which she seems quite sure that Mrs. Ripley was married in Fay House, in her mother's parlour." See Elizabeth Dana, letter to Vivien May Norris, February 17, 1900.

19. George Ripley, letter to Marianne Ripley from Cambridge, May 3, 1826, as quoted in O.B. Frothingham, *George Ripley* ("American Men of Letters," ed. C. D. Warner; Boston and New York, Houghton, Mifflin and Co., 1882), p. 34.

20. "Notes of an interview with Miss Elizabeth Dana, 15 Appian Way, made by Miss Rose Sherman, in 1928."

21. This crayon portrait was made from a photograph taken of Mrs. Ripley during her last illness. Her husband did not think it a good likeness. He gave it to the Sisters of the Good Shepherd. See George Ripley, letter to R. H. Dana, Sr., June 11, 1861, (now in Massachusetts Historical Society, Dana Collection). The portrait was in the possession of the Convent of the Good Shepherd, "Villa Loretto," Peekskill, New York, the sisters had it in 1948. It now appears to be lost. H. D. R. 1993.

22. Isabella Dana of Boston, letter to Miss Elizabeth Dana of Cambridge, October 1928. The quotations used were sent to Miss Rose Sherman in 1928 by Elizabeth Dana and are now in the possession of Radcliffe College. The original letter from Isabella Dana seems to have been lost.

23. John Thomas Codman, *Brook Farm, Historic and Personal Memoirs* (Boston: Arena Publishing Co., 1894), p. 17: "In person she was tall, slender and graceful, with rather light, smooth hair, worn in the plain style of the day. Being near-sighted she was obliged to use a glass when looking at a distant person or thing. I do not know at what age Sophia started to wear a glass."

Jon van der Zee Sear, My Friends at Brook Farm (New York: Desmond Fitzgerald, Inc., 1912), p. 70:

"Mrs. Ripley, born Sophia Dana, was a slender, graceful lady."

24. Codman, op. cit., p. 17: "Her manner was vivacious and she was a good conversationalist."

Sears, op.cit., p. 70: "...charming in manner, animated and blithe."

25. Isaac Hecker, "Tribute to Mrs. George Ripley," Hecker Papers XXXI (Paulist Fathers Archives, New York City).

26. Marianne Dwight, *Letters from Brook Farm 1844–1847*, ed. Amy L. Reed (Poughkeepsie: Vassar College, 1928), p. 3: "Mrs Ripley ran across the room to us."

27. Sophia Willard Ripley, letter to Lydia Hobart Ripley, February 17, 1831: "I ran down into the study to warm myself, after flying, or trotting round as usual...."

28. *House Journal of Massachusetts General Court May 1829–March 1830* (Massachusetts State Library, Boston). We have very little information about this Francis Dana except from members of the family who suffered from his financial ventures, and from Sophia Willard Dana Ripley, with whom he was apparently very uncongenial. Ruth Charlotte Dana, who is the source for much of the information, was Sophia's intimate friend, and might well have been prejuidiced against Francis. Some citizens of Middlesex County must have liked him, since they elected him to the Legislature. Given the information about his prodigality and the straitened condition of the family exchequer, it is amusing to find that Francis Dana introduced a bill to permit himself and some other men to beautify Cambridge Common with planting and other landscaping at their own expense. See House Journal, pp. 375, 401–402. Also Lucius R. Paige, History of Cambridge Massachusetts 1630–1877 (Boston: H.D. Houghton anc Co.; New York: Hurd and Houghton, 1877). He was also appointed one of the Commissioners to examine the accounts of Joseph Sewall, Treasurer and Receiver General of Massachusetts: See House Journal, p. 36.

29. George Ripley, letter to Marianne Ripley, May 3, 1826, as quot-

ed in Frothingham, George Ripley, pp. 33–34.

30. Frothingham, op. cit., p. 45.

31. Sophia Willard Dana Ripley, letters to Lydia Hobart Ripley. Most of the letters are dated by day of the week and day of the month only. I have tried to figure out the years with the help of a perpetual calendar and from internal evidence in the letters. Where the dating is mine I have enclosed it in brackets.

32. Sophia Willard Dana Ripley, letter to Lydia Hobart Ripley, Wednesday, August 4, [1830].

33. Letter: Monday, March 30, [1829].

34. Sophia Willard Dana Ripley, letter to Lydia Hobart Ripley, Wednesday, August 4, [1830].

35. John Quincy Adams served as secretary to Francis Dana Sr. when the latter went to Russia to the court of Catherine the Great. He was only fifteen at the time. He named his son Charles Francis Adams, in honor of Francis Dana. See Dana, The Dana Saga, p. 31.

36. Sophia Willard Dana Ripley, letter to Lydia Hobart Ripley, Tuesday, November 2, [1830].

37. Sophia Willard Dana Ripley, letter to Lydia Hobart Ripley, Saturday, October 23, [1830].

38. Sophia Willard Dana Ripley, letter to Lydia Hobart Ripley, January 26, [1831].

39. Sophia Willard Dana Ripley, letter to Lydia Hobart Ripley, Saturday, February 19, 1831.

40. Sophia Willard Dana Ripley, letter to Lydia Hobart Ripley from Boston, Monday, February 6, 1832. This refernce throws light and helps to date a visit of Longfellow's to Boston, about which very little is known.

41. Frothingham, George Ripley, p. 54.

42. Frothingham, George Ripley, pp. 110–111.

43. R. W. Emerson, "An Address," delivered before the Senior Class in Divinity College, Cambridge, Sunday evening, July 15, 1838. The Works of Ralph Wald Emerson, Standard Library Edition (Boston: Houghton, Mifflin and Company, 1883), I, 119–148. Among other bombshells he cooly let drop the following: "The sublime is excited in me by the great stoical doctrine, Obey thyself. That which shows God in me, fortifies me. That which shows God out of me, makes me a wart and a wen. There is no longer a necessary reason for my being."

44. See, for example, Elizabeth Peabody, "A Glimpse of Christ's Ideal of Society," *The Dial*, II, no. 2 (October, 1841), pp. 214–228.

45. Quoted in Frothingham, *George Ripley*, p. 111.

46. "Letter," *The Dial*, II, no. 1 (July, 1841), pp. 122–129. Reprinted in The New Yorker, IX (July 17, 1841), with change of title to "A Western Community." Sophia Ripley always published anonymously.

George Willis Cooke established the authorship of her articles in The Dial. See his "The Dial': an Historical and Biographical Introduction, with a list of the contributors," *Journal of Speculative Philosophy*, XIX, no. 3 (July, 1885), pp. 225–265.

47. Sophia Ripley's nephew, Frank Dana was born 1835. His birthday was the occasion of a party in the woods at Brook Farm in 1841. See Nathaniel Hawthorne, *Passages from the American Notebooks* (Boston and New York: Houghton, Mifflin & Co., 1886), entry for September 28, 1841, p. 251.

48. A criticism of realism by a Transcendentalist! To try to "idealize the actual" was characteristic of the Transcendentalists.

49. Cristopher Pearce Cranch, poet, artist, satirist, musician, He studied for the ministry and graduated from the Harvard Divinity School a year ahead of Dwight. He and Dwight both abandoned the ministry.

50. Anna G. Alvord, who later built "The Cottage" at Brook Farm.

51. Marianne Ripley, George Ripley's sister.

52. Margaret Fuller's "Conversations" were famous. See Caroline W. Healey, *Margaret and her Friends* (Boston: Roberts others, 1895), *passim*.

53. Ralph Waldo Emerson.

54. Emerson?.

55. William Ellery Channing.

56. Probably Cornelius Conway Felton, classical scholar, professor of Greek and Latin at Harvard. He was a close friend of Emerson, Longfellow and Hawthorne.

57. Popular vocalists. Henry Russell wrote "The Ivy Green," "The Old Arm Chair," "A Life on the Ocean Wave," "Some Love to Roam," "Woodman Spare that Tree," He liked to recite soliloquies from Hamlet and Macbeth. After reading Sophia's description of his style one shudders to think what he must have done to those characters.

58. A famous Boston mission preacher, sometimes called "the sailor preacher." His Protestentism was of an orthodox variety—which gave spice to the anecdote.

59. Probably Dr. Cyrus Augustus Bartel.

60. H. W .L. Dana, *Dana Family Genealogy*, soon to be published.

61. Sophia Williard Dana Ripley, letter to John Sullivan Dwight, Sunday [February 9, 1840] (Boston Public Library, Dwight Collection).

62. Sophia Willard Dana Ripley, letter to John Sullivan Dwight, from West Roxury, August 1, 1840 (Boston Pulic Library, Dwigt Collection).

63. George Ripley, letter to the parishioners of the Purchase Street Church, October 1, 1840. Quoted in Forthingham, *George Ripley*, pp.

63–91.

64. "I have no faith in the efficacy or lawfulness of public or private wars." Ibid, p. 88.

65. Frothingham, *opus cit.*, p. 91.

66. Sophia Willard Dana Ripley, letter to John Sullivan Dwight, Thursday, May 6, [1841] (Boston Public Library, Dwight Collection).

67. It is quoted in connection with Brook Farm by Isaac Hecker. See his *Questions of the Soul* (New York: D. Appleton and Company, 1855), p. 23.

68. Sophia Willard Dana Ripley, letter to John Sullivan Dwight, May 6, [1841] (Boston Public Lirary, Dwight Collection). The statements below are from the same letter.

69. Quoted in Lindsay Swift, *Brook Farm* (New York: Macmillan Company, 1900), pp. 15–16.

70. They are given in Frothingham, *George Ripley*, pp. 112–115.

71. Elizabeth Palmer Peabody, "Plan of the West Roxbury Community," *The Dial*, II, no. 3 (January, 1842), pp. 361–372.

72. Katherine Burton pointed this out in the introduction to her *Paradise Planters* (New York: Longmans, Green & Co. 1939).

73. See footnote 71.

74. Nathaniel Hawthorne, *Passages from the American Notebooks* (Boston: Houghton, Mifflin & Co., 1886), p. 3. Entry for June 1, 1841: "In the midst of toil, or after a hard day's work in the gold-mine [Hawthorne's 'idealization of the actual' for the manure pile], my soul ostinately refused to be poured out on paper....It is my opinion that a man's soul may be buried and perish under a dung-heap, or in a furrow of the field, just as well as under a pile of money."

75. Ameilia Russell, *Home Life of the Brook Farm Association* (Boston: Little, Brown and Co., 1900), pp. 10–11. Also George P. Bradford, "Reminiscences of Brook Farm by a memer of the Community," Century Magazine, XLV, no. 1 (Novemer , 1872), p. 144.

76. Bradford, *op. cit.*, 144. Also Ora Gennet Sedgwick, "A Girl of Sixteen at Brook Farm," *Atlantic Monthly*, LXXV (March, 1900), p. 399.

77. Sedgwick, *op. cit.*, p. 399.

78. Bradford, *op. cit.*, p. 148.

79. Sedgwick, *op. cit.*, p. 399.

80. Georgianna Bruce Kiry, *Years of Experience* (New York: G. P. Puthnam's Sons, 1887), pp. 89–90.

81. Frothingham, *George Ripley*, p. 115.

82. Russell, *Home Life of the Brook Farm Association*, p. 63.

83. Bradford, "Reminiscences of Brook Farm y a member of the Community," p. 144.

84. *Op. cit.*, pp. 146–147.

85. The reminiscences of former students at Brook Farm are quite

rhapsodic. Perhaps Ora Gannet Sedgwick analysed the school best when she said: "the teaching at Brook Farm was fine, and, to one who really wished to learn, of the very best kind." See Sedgwick, "A Girl of Sixteen at Brook Farm," p. 400. Material on the school I have collected from the various memoirs and reminiscences cited in the bibliography. For the best secondary account see Swift, Brook Farm, pp. 69–84. It includes a letter written by Georgianna Bruce Kirby while she was at Brook Farm.

86. John Van der Zee Sears, *My Friends at Brook Farm* (New York: Desmond Fitzgerald, Inc., 1912), p.113: "Care of the cow being regarded as a disagreeable duty, Dr. Ripley took it upon himself, just as Mrs. Ripley took the scrubbing of the kitchen floor. Mrs. Ripley had other little matters to look after, general oversight of the girls, teaching Greek, entertaining distinguished guests, writing clever musical plays for the Festal Series, etc., but she kept the floor clean all the same." This is the only evidence I have found that Mrs. Ripley ever taught Greek.

87. Sophia Ripley, "Women," *The Dial*, I, no. 3 (January, 1841), pp. 36–366.

88. Sophia Ripley, "Painting and Sculpture," *The Dial*, II, no. 1 (July, 1841), p. 122–129.

89. Russell, *Home Life of the Brook Farm Association*, pp. 20–21.

90. Ibid., p. 21–22.

91. See p. 10 of this essay.

92. Kirby, *Years of Experience*, p. 99.

93. Ibid., p. 172. "She was gentle, refined, well informed, but narrow and, compared to others, artificial. While you were in her mood, or state of mind, she accepted you with all amiability; when you were groping in the dark, or tempest-tossed, she helplessly abandoned you to your fate, perhaps condemned you, as those always condemn who are incapable of understanding others.... Sophia was a mother to the little ones, and they loved her accordingly,. *Their* affairs were simple enough. She did more than her duty, while with others love obliterated duty. She endured the repulsive and uncongenial for the sake of principle: *we* knew not duty." For Sophia Ripley's opinion of Georgianna, see her letter to Margaret Fuller, pp. 59–61 of this essay.

94. Ibid., p. 21.

95. Marianne Dwight, *Letters From Brook Farm*, ed. Amy L. Reed (Poughkeepsie: Vassar College, 198), p. 3.

96. Ibid., 172. Marianne had been highly indignant because Mrs. Ripley wanted her to quarantine her sister Fanny, when the latter was taken ill during a smallpox epidemic at Brook Farm. This suggests some of the exasperation the Ripleys must have undergone in coping with Transcendentalist temperments.

97. Margaret Fuller to William Henry Channing, from Jamaica

Plain, January 1, 1840 (Boston Public Library, Channing Collection).

98. Isaac Hecker, "Tribute to Mrs. George Ripley." Manuscript, Hecker Papers, XXXI a (Paulist Fathers Archives, New York). Given in full in the Appendix to this essay.

99. Charles Anderson Dana.

100. Sophia Willard Dana Ripley, letter to Ralph Waldo Emerson July 5, [1843, year written in Emerson's hand]. (Houghton Library, Harvard University, Emerson Papers).

101. Sophia Willard Dana Ripley, letter to Ralph Waldo Emerson, July 29, [1843 year written in Emerson's hand] (Houghton Library, Harvard University, Emerson Papers).

102. Hawthorne, *Passages from the American Notebooks*, p. 25.

103. See p. 26 of this essay.

104. Sophia Willard Dana Ripley, letter to Margaret Fuller (Houghton Library, Harvard University, Fuller Papers).

105. George Ripley.

106. Charles A. Dana.

107. Georgianna Bruce.

108. Sophia Willard Dana Ripley, letter to Margaret Fuller (Houghton Library, Harvard University, Fuller Papers).

109. Quoted in Kirby, *Years of Experience*, p. 178. The original letter has been lost.

110. Russell, *Home Life of the Brook Farm Association*, pp. 72–76.

111. Quoted in Russell, *Home Life of the Brook Farm Association*, pp. 78–80.

112. Russell, *Home Life of the Brook Farm Association*, p. 105.

113. Sophia Willard Dana Ripley, letter to Ruth Charlotte Dana, September 12, 1846. (Massachusetts Historical Society, Dana Collection.)

114. Sophia Willard Dana Ripley, letter to Henry Wadsworth Longfellow, October 20, 1847 (Longfellow House, Cambridge).

115. Dwight, Letters from Brook Farm, p. 21.

116. John Codman, *Brook Farm, Historic and Personal Memoirs*, (Boston: Arena Publishing Co., 1894), p. 198.

117. Dwight, *Letters from Brook Farm*, p. 147.

118. Russell, *Home Life of the Brook Farm Association*, p. 26.

119. Robert F. Metzdorf, "Hawthorne's Suit Against Ripley and Dana," *American Literature*, XII, no. 2, (May, 1940). Reprint unpaged.

120. Sophia Willard Dana Ripley, letter to John Sullivan Dwight, Saturday, March 14, 1846 (Boston: Public Library, Dwight Collection).

121. Dwight, Letters from Brook Farm, p. 172.

122. Ibid, p. 166.

123. Sophia Willard Dana Ripley, letter to Ruth Charlotte Dana,

September 12, 1846.

124. Sophia Willard Dana Ripley, letter to Henry Wadsworth Longfellow, October 20, 1847, (Longfellow House, Cambridge).

125. Swift, *Brook Farm*, p. 145.

126. See p. 56–57 of this essay.

127. Sophia Willard Dana Ripley, letter to Ruth Charlotte Dana, September 12, 1846 (Massachusetts Historical Society, Dana Collection).

128. Probably Horace Sumner, younger brother of Charles Sumner.

129. Orestes Augustus Brownson.

130. Sophia Willard Dana Ripley, letter to Ruth Charlotte Dana, May 10, [1848] (Massachusetts Historical Society, Dana Collection).

131. Perhaps John Sullivan Dwight?

132. John Cheever was an eccentric Irishman at Brook Farm. It was rumored that he was the natural son of a baronet. His greatest talent was exposing hypocrites! Perhaps Mrs. Ripley meant he would understand she was in earnest.

133. Sophia Willard Dana Ripley, letter to Ruth Charlotte Dana, September 3, 1847 (Massachusetts Historical Society, Dana Collection).

134. The archivist of the Archdiocese of New York, Father Brennan, has no records of baptisms so far back.

135. Sophia Willard Dana Ripley, letter to Henry Wadsworth Longfellow, January 23, 1848, mistakenly dated by Sophia, 1847 (Longfellow House, Cambridge).

136. William Henry Channing, "Ernest the Seeker," *The Dial*, I, nos. 1 and 2 (July and October, 1840), pp. 48–58; 233–242.

137. Swift, *Brook Farm*, p. 218.

138. Isaac Hecker, "Tribute to Mrs. George Ripley," manuscript, Hecker Papers, XXXIa (Paulist Fathers Archives, New York City). Given in full in the Appendix of this essay. Father Hecker said he did not know Mrs. Ripley well at this time.

139. George Ripley, letter to Richard Henry Dana Sr., March 3, 1861 (Massachusetts Historical Society, Dana Collection).

140. Sophia Willard Dana Ripley, letter to Ruth Charlotte Dana, March, 1848 (Massachusetts Historical Society, Dana Collection).

141. *Ibid,*; the underscoring is mine.

142. Abbe Martinet, *Religion in Society or the Solution of Great Problems; Placed within the Reach of Every Mind*, translated from the French of the Abbe Martinet (New York: D. and J. Sadlier, 1850). This book was translated anonymously. Sadlier, the publishers, have no record of the translator. There are several reasons for attributing it to Mrs. Ripley: (1) in her letter to Brownson she speaks of the book she is translating as "des Grands Problemes"; (2) the date of publication conincides with the date of Mrs. Ripley's book; (3) Bishop Hughes wrote the Introduction

and Mrs. Ripley in a letter to Ruth Charlotte Dana, August 5, 1849 says the Bishop is reading the book preparatory to writing the Introduction; (4) the "translator's note" says two more volumes will follow. In her letter to Brownson Mrs. Ripley says that she intends to publish the first two volumes first; (5) the book deals with subjects in which Mrs. Ripley was interested, and answers her description of the book. For some reason Brownson did not write a preface.

143. Frothingham, *George Ripley*, p. 237; Swift, *Brook Farm*, p. 142.

144. Brownson Papers, University of Notre Dame.

145. Compare Isaac Hecker's analysis of the reasons for Mrs. Ripley's conversion in his "Tribute to Mrs. George Ripley" in the Appendix of this essay.

146. George Ripley, letter to John Sullivan Dwight, November 8, 1847 (Boston Public Library, Dwight Collection).

147. Unless otherwise stated, information in this chapter is from a series of Letters from Sophia Willard Dana Ripley to Ruth Charlotte Dana 1847–180 (Massachusetts Historical Society, Dana Collection).

148. Sophia Willard Dana Ripley, letter to Ruth Charlotte Dana, [June 7, 1848].

149. Sophia Willard Dana Ripley, letter to Ruth Charlotte Dana, [March, 1848].

150. *Ibid*, [April 27, 1848].

151. *Ibid*, May 1, 1848. Sophia took the name Elizabeth, when she was confirmed July 9, [1849] and thereafter added it to her signature. See her letter of July 18, [1848].

152. *Ibid*., April 29, 1849.

153. *Ibid*., May 25, [1849].

154. Sophia Willard Dana Ripley, letter to Ruth Charlotte Dana, May 1, [1848].

155. *Ibid*., [June 7, 1848].

156. *Ibid*, May 1, [1848].

157. Sophia Willard Dana Ripley, letter to Ruth Charlotte Dana, [March, 1849] (Massachusetts Historical Society, Dana Collection).

158. *Ibid*.

159. Sophia Willard Dana Ripley, letter to Ruth Charlotte Dana, [March, 1848].

160. Ibid,, August 5, [1849].

161. Sophia Willard Dana Ripley, letter to Ruth Charlotte Dana, [March, 1850].

162. Letter to Ruth Charlotte Dana, Sept. 3, 1847.

163. See above, p. 82.

164. Sophia Willard Dana Ripley, letter to Ruth Charlotte Dana, December 2, [1853].

165. *Ibid*., December 6, [1857].

166. George Ripley, letter to Orestes Brownson, June 22, 1848 (Notre Dame University, Brownson Papers). Acccording to Sophia's letters she thought George's heart drawing nearere to the Catholic Church during the succeeding years, but not his intellect. But she believed he would ultimately be converted. See especially Sophia Willard Dana Ripley to Ruth Charlotte Dana, December 6, 1857. She also wrote: "Father Hecker thinks Mr. R- is pursuing the right course, which I have never doubted in the main, & he knows more about it than anyone else." See *Ibid.*, December 2, 1853. This is important contemporary evidence, because Hecker and Brownson, looking back many years later, said publicly that they thought George Ripley was only deterred from becoming Catholic during this period by worldly considerations. Possibly their memories betrayed them. Possibly they had spoken evidence unavailable to us. Or possibly George Ripley may have made a joking remark which they took seriously. He had a habit of making such jokes. See p. 96 of this essay. For Hecker's and Brownson's statements see Howard Aaron WIlson, "George Ripley: Social and Literary Critic" (unpublished Ph.D. dissertation, University of Wisconsin, 1941), pp. 194–199. I have found no evidence to support Hecker and Brownson's impression in George Ripley's letters, but rather a growing uncertainty on religious matters.

167. S. W. D. Ripley, letter to Ruth Charlotte Dana, August 5, [1849].

168. *Ibid.*, May 17, [1848].

169. *Ibid.*, August 5, [1849].

170. *Ibid.*, April 1851.

171. *Ibid.*, September 18, [1857] and December 6, [1857].

172. Frothingham, *George Ripley*, p. 199.

173. Though certain aspects of Fourierism were very akin to Catholicisim. For instance, the belief in the solidarity of the human race. Isaac Hecker wrote Brownson on April 6, 1844: "The doctrine of unity and diversity of action in the industrial world as held out by these men what is it but Catholicity in the industrial world?" (Notre Dame University, Brownson Papers).

174. Bishop Hughes told her she must go "as the companion of my husband." See Sophia Willard Dana Ripley, letter to Ruth Charlotte Dana, April 9, 1848.

175. Sophia Willard Dana Ripley, letter to Ruth Charlotte Dana, April 1, 1848.

176. *Ibid.*, May 25, 1849. Mount St. Vincent Academy in those days occupied the site that is now the north end of Central Park in New York.

177. *Ibid.*, September 26, 1850.

178. *Ibid.*, April 29, 1849.

179. See, for example her letter to Ruth Charlotte Dana, January 12, [1850]: "...a visit to the Rev. Mother & Sisters at St. Catharine's...Oh! It was so sweet! their childlike ways, & her gentle, maternal manners."

180. Letter to R.C. Dana, Palm Sunday [1857]. Also February 17, 1852. The popes use this signature.

181. George Ripley, letter to John Sullivan Dwight, March 26, 1849 (Boston Public Library, Dwight Collection).

182. *Ibid.*, April 6, 1849.

183. Sophia Willard Dana Ripley, letter to Ruth Charlotte Dana, April 29, 1849.

184. Copy of letter from Isaac Hecker in Sophia Ripley's writing, sent by her to Ruth Charlotte Dana. Also letter from Sophia Willard Dana Ripley to Ruth Charlotte Dana, (October 1851 saying her new book is going to press; hope is "will be worthy of our blessed Lady & St. Alphonsus." An English translation did appear that year.)

185. Sophia Willard Dana Ripley, letter to Ruth Charlotte Dana, January 12, [1850].

186. *Ibid.*, July 14, 1850.

187. *Life and Doctrine of Saint Catherine of Genoa*, trans. from Italian (New York: The Catholic Publication Society Co., 1874). For statements that the translation was by Mrs. Ripley, consult the preface to the book written by Father Hecker, now in typewritten copy (Paulist Fathers Archives, New York), and Caryl Coleman, "A Forgotten Convert," *Catholic World*, CXXII (October–March, 1925–1926), p. 202.

188. *Life and Doctrine of Saint Catherine of Genoa*, Introduction, pp. 16–17.

189. Sophia Willard Dana Ripley, letters to Ruth Charlotte Dana, passim. Also Isaac Hecker, "Tribute to Mrs. George Ripley" given in Appendix to this essay.

190. Katherine E. Conway, *In the Footprints of the Good Shepherd*, (New York: Convent of the Good Shepherd, 1907), pp. 37–38.

191. Sophia Willard Dana Ripley, letters to Ruth Charlotte Dana, 1857–1860, *passim*. Also Conway, In the Fottprints of the Good Shepherd, pp. 34–47.

192. Conway, *In the Footprints of the Good Shepherd*, p. 79.

193. Sophia Willard Dana Ripley, letter to Ruth Charlotte Dana, December 22, [1853]. In a postscript Sophia wrote: "Mr. Ripley has just come in & is decidedly in favor of very decided measures. It is the first time I have spoken to him of the painful cause of our distress."

194. *Ibid.*, October 20, [1853].

195. Frothingham, *George Ripley*, p. 237.

196. Sophia Willard Dana Ripley, letters to Ruth Charlotte Dana, August 2, [1860]; and to Richard Henry Dana, Sr., August 17, 1860. (Both letters at Massachusetts Historical Society, Dana Collection.)

197. Sophia Willard Dana Ripley, letter to Ruth Charlotte Dana, September 30, [1860].

198. George Ripley, letter to R. H. Dana, Sr. and to Ruth Charlotte Dana, 1861–1862 (Massachusetts Historical Society, Dana Collection).

199. George Ripley, letter to R. H.Dana, Sr., March 3, 1861.

200. Frothingham, *George Ripley*, p. 239.

201. George Ripley, letter to Elizabeth Ellery Dana, February 18, 1861 (Massachusetts Historical Society, Dana Collection).

202. George Ripley, letter to R. H. Dana, Sr., March 3, 1861. I have changed the order of the quotation slightly. The last sentence came at the beginning.

203. Hecker Papers XXXIa (Paulist Fathers Archives, New York City).

204. This visit occurred in 1844, not 1845. Father Hecker became a Catholic in 1844.

205. Father Hecker seems to have become Mrs. Ripley's confessor in 1851.

Index